a **WEE GUIDE** *to*
the Haunted Castles
of Scotland

a **WEE GUIDE** *to*

the Haunted Castles *of* Scotland

Martin Coventry

GOBLINSHEAD

Edinburgh

a **WEE GUIDE** to the Haunted Castles of Scotland

First Published 1996
Reprinted 1997
© Martin Coventry 1996

Published by **GOBLINSHEAD**
12 Merchiston Crescent
Edinburgh EH10 5AS
Scotland

British Library Cataloguing in Publication Data
A catalogue record for this book is available from the British Library.

ISBN 1 899874 05 4

Typeset by **GOBLINSHEAD** using Desktop Publishing
Typeset in Garamond Narrow

WEE GUIDES

Already published July 1997
Scottish History
Haunted Castles of Scotland
William Wallace
Mary, Queen of Scots
Robert Burns
Robert the Bruce
Old Churches and Abbeys of Scotland

Planned for late 1997/8
Castles and Historic Houses of Scotland
Bonnie Prince Charlie
Whisky
The Picts

a **WEE GUIDE** *to*
the Haunted Castles
of Scotland

Contents

List of illustrations	i
Acknowledgements	ii
How to use this book	iii
Introduction	iv
Haunted castles of Scotland	1
List of haunted castles	7
Glossary of terms	82
Index	84

List of illustrations

Claypotts Castle	3	Duntrune Castle	44
Edinburgh Castle	5	Eilean Donan Castle	47
Map locating all the castles	8-9	Fyvie Castle	50
Duntulm Castle	10	Glamis Castle	52
Abergeldie Castle	11	Holyrood Palace	55
Ardrossan Castle	13	Huntingtower Castle	56
Ballindalloch Castle	16	Inveraray Castle	57
Borthwick Castle	19	Kellie Castle	59
Braemar Castle	20	Kindrochit Castle	60
Brodick Castle	22	Lauriston Castle	61
Castle Grant	25	Linlithgow Palace	62
Castle of Moy	27	Lordscairnie Castle	64
Cawdor Castle	28	Melgund Castle	67
Corgarff Castle	30	Neidpath Castle	69
Craignethan Castle	33	Roslin Castle	73
Crathes Castle	34	Skibo Castle	77
Culzean Castle	37	Stirling Castle	78
Duart Castle	39	Taymouth Castle	80
Dunnottar Castle	40	Traquair House	80
Dunrobin Castle	42		

Acknowledgements

Thanks to the National Trust for Scotland for their permission to reproduce the photograph of Culzean Castle (page 37).

Many thanks to Joyce Miller – who looked over the manuscript, and had the dubious honour of proofreading it – for her photo of Neidpath Castle (page 69) and to Helen Fraser, my comrade in arms in castle hunting. Also to Gilbert Ellice, without whom this would never have happened.

How to use this book

This book is divided into two main parts:

- The first part (pages 1-6) is a brief overview of the development of the castle in Scotland, and then goes on to examine themes common to some of the ghost stories.
- The second part (pages 7-83) lists over 130 castles, said to have been haunted at some time. A map, covering two pages (pages 8–9), locates every castle. Each entry begins with the name of the castle, its location, and then its National Grid Reference and Ordnance Sheet Landranger number. This is followed by a description of the ghost story, and any other interesting tales. The final part covers opening – where available and applicable – with telephone numbers and facilities, including parking, refreshments, sales area, admission, WC, and disabled facilities

  A glossary of terms (pages 82-3) concludes this part

An index (pages 84-6) lists all the main people and events alphabetically.

Warning

While the information in this book was believed to be correct at time of going to press – and was checked, where possible, with the visitor attractions – opening times and facilities, or other information, may vary or differ from that included. All information should be checked with the visitor attractions before embarking on any journey. Inclusion in the text is no indication whatsoever that a site is open to the public or that it should be visited. Many sites, particularly ruined castles, are potentially dangerous and great care should be taken: the publisher and author cannot accept responsibility for damage or injury caused from any visit.

The places listed to visit are only a personal selection of what is available in Scotland, and the inclusion or exclusion of a visitor attraction in the text should not be considered as a comment or judgement on that attraction.

Locations on the map are approximate.

Introduction

This wee book came about because of two unrelated events. The first was a review of *The Castles of Scotland* book, which pointed out that many of the stories associated with castles appeared to involve corporeal and non-corporeal spirits. With due thought and consideration, I decided a whole publication dedicated to this might be worthwhile.

The second event was a media producer from the USA getting in touch about haunted castles, as he was intending to make a documentary. This sent me searching through my mind trying to recollect stories of *Green Ladies* and ghostly cannonballs, headless Comyns and suffocating Ogilvies, handless pipers and spectral drummers. It then occurred to me how many castles were reputedly haunted. So, combining my new found obsession for macabre stories, and my old obsession with castles, I busied myself writing this book.

I – personally – have had no supernatural experiences in any castle, just creepy feelings in the later house – in the WC, oddly enough – in the courtyard at Craignethan, in the *Green Room* at Crathes, and at the chapel near Dunstaffnage Castle. I know, however, that many do believe in ghosts, including many of those who own or inhabit castles – and I have no reason to disbelieve them. My own only definite experience of unusual phenomena is limited to thumping sounds in a council house in Warrington, while working in England, and any logical or scientific – or even supernatural – explanation eludes me.

I hope the reading of this book is as much fun as the writing of it. Nothing recorded in the following pages, however, is meant to either affirm or deny the existence of bogles and spirits – it is up to the reader to decide. And if you know of any hauntings not included, please let me know.

MC, Edinburgh, November 1996

Haunted Castles of Scotland

The following book is about castles and about ghosts. No self respecting castle is without its own bogle, and many have two or three, or whole parties of Ogilvies crying out their last, locked in an airless chamber. Many have been continuously occupied since medieval times, others stand on the sites of Iron Age fortifications dating back even further. What is also true is that these strongholds saw more than their fair share of cruel and bloody deeds. The Scottish nobility – like others of the time from other countries – were a wild and lawless lot, and their treatment of their own families and servants was often as vicious as their dealings with their bitterest enemies.

Many of the castles covered are open to the public, either as private homes, in the care of Historic Scotland or the National Trust for Scotland, or as a pile of rubble – and where possible this is indicated in the text. A few are hotels. Others, however, are not open and care should be taken, more from corporeal landowners than malevolent spirits. Where possible opening times have been checked along with information on location and facilities.

However, it should be said that nothing in this book suggests any manifestation is likely to occur, and nothing included affirms or denies the existence of ghosts. Some of the stories are relatively well documented – the manifestations can be linked to the death of a specific person, usually by murder or suicide, and it is after this that disturbances began. It should also be said that many stories appealed to the Victorian idea of romance and horror – and many have been embellished over the years. For others, there is little or no information about hauntings – or who or what caused them.

The use or non-use of words such as *reputed*, *reported* or *it is said* has no significance.

The Development of the Scottish Castle

The main function of the castle was defensive, to protect the lord and his family from their enemies, in as comfortable surroundings as possible; but the castle was also an administrative centre, where rents were collected and justice dispensed. The castle was both a show of the lord's wealth, prestige and power, and a symbol of his authority.

The earliest fortified sites consisted of hill forts, brochs and duns, dating

1

from before recorded history. Some of these were occupied as late as the 17th century – and the sites of many others were reused for later fortresses. Hill forts are found all over Scotland, but brochs and duns tend to be concentrated in the north and west. These were the first castles, permanently occupied strongholds at the centre of relatively fertile lands.

After the Battle of Hastings in 1066, motte and bailey castles were introduced to Scotland – although they are unevenly distributed, being particularly numerous in Galloway, where there were rebellions in later centuries. Two survivors from this type of defence are Duffus Castle, although the motte was not strong enough for the later stone keep, and Rothesay Castle. Royal castles were built in areas where the king's authority was challenged, and this also continued into the following centuries.

By the 13th century, the motte and bailey had been superseded by castles of enclosure, where a site was surrounded by a strong stone wall encircling timber or stone buildings – this offered better protection against fire. Castle Sween, Castle Tioram and Mingary Castle all have enclosing walls dating from this time.

Some of these fortresses were developed into large castles with massive keeps, gatehouses and towers. Bothwell, Caerlaverock, Kildrummy and Dirleton all date substantially from this time. Other large fortresses did not survive the Wars of Independence, as it was Robert the Bruce's policy to destroy strongholds so that they could not be held by the English. Besides, large stone castles were expensive to build and maintain, and in the late 14th and 15th centuries simple keeps were built, usually with a small enclosure or courtyard.

Some strong Royal castles were maintained, including those at Edinburgh, Stirling, Roxburgh, Dumbarton and Dunbar; and a few of the most powerful families could also afford massive fortresses, such as the Douglas strongholds of Tantallon and Threave, and the Keith stronghold of Dunnottar.

The keep evolved into the tower house, which was not as massive or simple, and had more regard to comfort. Hundreds of these towers were built in the 16th century, particularly in the Border area. During the later 16th and 17th centuries, the simple rectangular tower house developed into L- and Z-plan tower houses, with added wings which provided more accommodation, covering fire and amenity. While few tower houses were built in the south of Scotland after the end of the 16th century, castles continued to be built and inhabited in the north of Scotland, although these were highly sophisticated structures, such as Crathes, Craigievar and Claypotts.

At the same time as nobles built and developed keeps and tower houses, the kings of Scots

Claypotts Castle – said to be haunted by a White Lady

built ornate, or refurbished, royal palaces. These were often developed out of older strongholds, but during the 15th and 16th centuries were remodelled in the Renaissance style to become comfortable residences. The palaces at Holyrood, Falkland, Linlithgow, Stirling and Dunfermline were all developed at this time.

As the need for defence decreased, many castles and tower houses were developed into mansion houses, such as Delgatie, Fyvie, Kellie; others were remodelled as barracks, such as Corgarff and Braemar; while others again were demolished and replaced by symmetrical mansions, such as Drumlanrig and Inveraray.

Castles and Ghosts

Nobody knows why apparitions and disturbances occur in particular locations, but certain factors seem to make this more likely. A violent death – either murder or suicide – appear to be the basis of many of the

3

stories, but there is also an element of injustice or guilt. A stone building or some other focus is also usually involved, disturbances sometimes being restricted to one room or stair or area. If the victim was a young woman, this also makes a haunting more likely. But why – considering there have been so many terrible acts of violence down the ages – so *few* castles and other buildings are haunted remains a mystery.

The tales can be divided into three rough areas. The first is women and men who died violently and unjustly; the second is men whose apparitions returned after death, characters simply too evil to rest; and the third heralds of events, sometimes good but usually bad, in a family, such as deaths and marriages.

By far the single largest number of reported apparitions and hauntings appear to have been the result of the deaths of young women – usually, but not in every case – in a violent manner. Many were murdered for becoming pregnant, for falling in love with the wrong man, or simply because they were the target for of a man's lust or jealousy. A few gentle souls died from a broken heart or committed suicide.

Some were concealed or walled up, as at Skibo, Castle Grant, Meggernie, Crathes and Fyvie, and the haunting seems to have been the only way to reveal their presence. Disturbances ceased when they were buried, although at Fyvie the haunting is said to have got worse when the remains were disturbed. Their appearance may have served as the conscience of those around them, who must have suspected foul play when a daughter or sister or friend disappeared.

A common theme is that the daughter of a laird fell in love with the wrong man, either someone far beneath her noble birth or the son of a bitter enemy. Not that marriage always resolved differences – the Gardners and Gardynes feuded for years after a wedding between their two families. Castle Grant, Cawdor, Kinnaird Head, Dunrobin, Ardblair and Newton, Neidpath and the Castle of Mey all have similar stories: the daughter of the house dies after being spurned or forbidden to see her lover, and her ghost returns to haunt the castle.

A related story to the young girl's downfall is an unwanted pregnancy, where she is then murdered, spurned or unable to cope with the unborn child. Borthwick Castle, Shieldhill, Crathes and the Castle of Park have stories of this kind. At Ackergill, Skibo, Meggernie, Mains Castle, Garth, Glamis, Sanquhar and Comlongon the young women died as the result of a man's lust, jealousy or cruelty, either killing herself to escape an unpleasant fate or being murdered or executed.

A few female apparitions – far fewer than male – are thought to be women involved in wrongdoing themselves, either murder or witchcraft or eloping with a lover. Abergeldie, Castle Cary, Castle Levan, Corstorphine, and Frendraught have tales of this kind.

In all this there are an unusually high proportion of *Green Ladies* – of all the castles included, 22 are said to have this colour of apparition. This may be because green was considered an unlucky colour in medieval times – being the colour of the fairies – but in most of the stories there is no reason given as why the apparition should wear this colour of gown. There are, however, also ten grey and eight white ladies, and one pink and two blue.

Another theme in stories concerns men too evil to rest in peace, some who also reputedly studied black arts or gamed with the devil.

At Glamis, *Earl Beardie*, Alexander Lindsay 4th Earl of Crawford is said to haunt a walled-up room where he played cards with the devil – although he is also said to be seen playing cards with the devil on the stroke of midnight of New Year's Eve at Lordscairnie Castle. Lord Soulis, a

Edinburgh Castle – once one of the foremost strongholds in Scotland, the castles is said to be haunted.

man of dark reputation, is said to haunt Hermitage; while the corpse of James Carnegie, 2nd Earl of Southesk, was reputedly was taken by a ghostly black coach driven by black horses from Kinnaird Castle. The shade of Alexander Stewart, Wolf of Badenoch, playing chess with the devil, reputedly haunts Ruthven. The house and grounds of The Binns are said to be haunted by the ghost of Tam Dalziel, who is also said to have played cards with the devil.

At Balnagown, the restless spirit of *Black* Andrew Munro is said to haunt the castle, after he was hanged from one of the windows for wrong doing. At Buckholm Tower, an apparition of the Pringle laird, who persecuted Covenanters, is said to be pursued by hounds; while at Carleton, Sir John Cathcart, who murdered several wives until murdered himself by his last, reputedly haunts the ruins. The *Bluidy Bruce,* Sir Andrew Bruce, another persecutor of Covenanters, is said to haunt Earlshall.

A third variation are heralds of death, births or marriage, these important life events. Barnbougle has a ghostly hound, heard when the laird is about to die, as does Noltland; Brodick, a white deer; Pitcaple, a robin. Cortachy Castle and Edinburgh, a ghostly drummer; Culzean, a piper; Dunstaffnage Castle, the *Ell-maid of Dunstaffnage*; Fyvie Castle, an apparition of Lilias Drummond, Huntingtower, a *Green Lady*. The headless rider, Ewen MacLaine, is said to herald a death in the MacLeans.

Some ghosts also seem to haunt more than one place. Not surprisingly considering all the castles and abbeys she visited while alive, apparitions of Mary, Queen of Scots are said to have been seen at Craignethan, Stirling, Loch Leven and Hermitage. Cardinal David Beaton appears at Ethie, Melgund, and possibly St Andrews; while Alexander Lindsay, 4th Earl of Crawford, is reputed to haunt Glamis and Lordscairnie. Lilias Drummond is said to haunt Fyvie and Pinkie; Jean Drummond Newton and Ardblair. Bonnie Prince Charlie Traquair and Culloden House, Lady Hamilton both Woodhouselee and Old Woodhouselee, and Porteous the miller moved from Spedlins Tower to Jardine Hall.

Without doubt, the following stories are only a selection of hauntings and disturbances in the many castles of Scotland. Others may come to light as more and more old tower houses are restored and reoccupied. After all, if a castle becomes ruined and nobody lives there, does the ghost still haunt the remains? Reputedly, perhaps.

THE CASTLES
(A–Z)

MAP NO & CASTLE	PAGE
1 Abergeldie Castle	11
2 Ackergill Tower	11
3 Aldourie Castle	12
4 Ardblair Castle	12
5 Ardrossan Castle	12
6 Ardvreck Castle	13
7 Ashintully Castle	14
8 Auchinvole House	14
9 Balcomie Castle	14
10 Baldoon Castle	15
11 Balgonie Castle	15
12 Ballindalloch Castle	16
13 Balmoral Castle	17
14 Balnagown Castle	17
15 Barcaldine Castle	17
16 Barnbougle Castle	18
17 Betlay Castle	18
18 The Binns	18
19 Borthwick Castle	19
20 Braco Castle	20
21 Braemar Castle	20
22 Brahan Castle	21
23 Brodick Castle	21
24 Buchanan Castle	22
25 Buckholm Tower	22
26 Carleton Castle	23
27 Caroline Park House	23
28 Castle Cary	23
29 Castle Coeffin	24
30 Castle Fraser	24
31 Castle Grant	25
32 Castle Levan	25
33 Castle Stuart	26
34 Castle of Mey	26
35 Castle of Moy	28
36 Castle of Park	28
37 Cawdor Castle	29
38 Cessnock Castle	29
39 Claypotts Castle	29
40 Cloncaird Castle	30
41 Comlongon Castle	30
42 Corgarff Castle	30
43 Coroghon Castle	31
44 Corstorphine Castle	31
45 Cortachy Castle	31
46 Craigcrook Castle	32
47 Craigievar Castle	32
48 Craignethan Castle	32
49 Cranshaws	33
50 Crathes Castle	34
51 Crichton Castle	35
52 Cromarty Castle	35
53 Culcreuch Castle	35
54 Cullen House	36
55 Culloden House	36
56 Culzean Castle	36
57 Dean Castle	37
58 Delgatie Castle	38
59 Drumlanrig Castle	38
60 Duart Castle	39
61 Duchal Castle	40
62 Dunnottar Castle	40
63 Dunphail Castle	41
64 Dunrobin Castle	42
65 Duns Castle	43
66 Dunstaffnage Castle	43
67 Duntrune Castle	43
68 Duntulm Castle	44
69 Durris House	45
70 Earlshall	45

Map place names: ORKNEY, Stornoway, Thurso, Wick, Elgin, Aberdeen, Inverness, Ullapool, Portree, SKYE, LEWIS, HARRIS, NORTH UIST, BENBECULA, SOUTH UIST, BARRA

107 Menie House 68
108 Muchalls Castle 68
109 Neidpath Castle 68
110 Newton Castle 69
111 Noltland Castle 70
112 Old Woodllee Cas 70
113 Penkaet Castle 71
114 Pinkie House 71
115 Pitcaple Castle 72
116 Rait Castle 72
117 Rockhall 72
118 Roslin Castle 73
119 Roxburgh Castle 74
120 Ruthven Barracks 74
121 Saddell Castle 74
122 St Andrews Castle 75
123 Saltoun Hall 75
124 Sanquhar Castle 76
125 Shieldhill 76
126 Skibo Castle 77
127 Spedlins Tower 77
128 Stirling Castle 78
129 Sundrum Castle 79
130 Taymouth Castle 79
131 Traquair House 79
132 Woodhouselee 80
133 Wemyss Castle 81

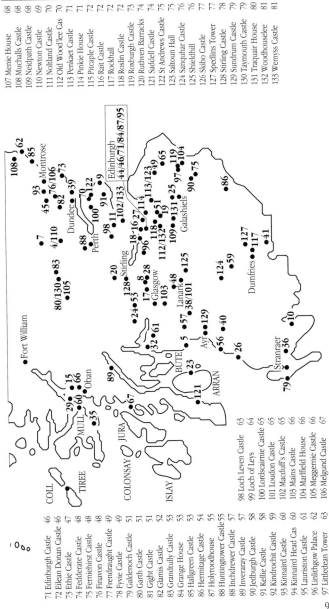

71 Edinburgh Castle 46
72 Eilean Donan Castle 46
73 Ethie Castle 47
74 Fedderate Castle 48
75 Ferniehirst Castle 48
76 Finavon Castle 48
77 Frendraught Castle 49
78 Fyvie Castle 49
79 Galdenoch Castle 51
80 Garth Castle 51
81 Gight Castle 51
82 Glamis Castle 52
83 Grandtully Castle 53
84 Grange House 53
85 Hallgreen Castle 53
86 Hermitage Castle 54
87 Holyroodhouse 55
88 Huntingtower Castle 55
89 Inveraray Castle 57
90 Jedburgh Castle 57
91 Kellie Castle 58
92 Kindrochit Castle 59
93 Kinnaird Castle 60
94 Kinnaird Head Cas 60
95 Lauriston Castle 61
96 Linlithgow Palace 62
97 Littledean Tower 63

98 Loch Leven Castle 63
99 Loch of Leys 64
100 Lordscairnie Castle 65
101 Loudon Castle 65
102 Macduff's Castle 65
103 Mains Castle 66
104 Marlfield House 66
105 Meggernie Castle 66
106 Melgund Castle 67

Key

P   Parking

S   Sales Area

☕   Refreshments

WC   Toilet

£   Admission Charge

♿   Disabled

HS   Historic Scotland

NTS   National Trust for Scotland

Numbers before entries refer to the map on page 8-9

Duntulm Castle – said to be haunted by so many ghosts that the MacDonald holders moved to a new house at Monkstadt.

1 Abergeldie Castle

Off B976, Abergeldie, 5 miles W of Ballater, Aberdeenshire
NO 287953   OS: 44

Abergeldie was held by the Gordons from 1482, although the tower, with its corbiestepped gables, dates mostly from the 16th century. It was leased to Queen Victoria in the 19th century, and then abandoned –

although it has since been restored and reoccupied.

The castle is said to be haunted by the spirit of a French maid, who was burnt at the stake after having been accused of witchcraft.

2 Ackergill Tower

Off A9, Ackergill, 2.5 miles N of Wick, Caithness
ND 352547   OS: 12

Ackergill Tower is a strong 15th-century castle of five storeys, which has a vaulted hall with a minstrels' gallery. It was remodelled by the architect David Bryce in 1851, and is still occupied.

The castle was probably built by the Keiths, although it passed from the family in the 17th century. The Keiths had a long running feud with the Gunns in the 15th century. The Gunns attacked the Keiths' lands, but were defeated at battles at Tannach Moor in 1438, and again at Dirlot in 1464. The chief of the Gunns and four of his sons were killed. In revenge, James Gunn slew Keith of Ackergill and his son, at Drummoy in 1518.

Caught up in all this was Helen Gunn of Braemore. Although betrothed to another, she was carried off by Dugald Keith of Ackergill, who desired her for himself. Rather than submit to him, she threw herself from the parapet of the castle and was killed. Her ghost, a *Green Lady*, is said to have been seen at the castle.

3 Aldourie Castle

Off B862, 8 miles SW of Inverness, Highland
NH 601372   OS: 26

A *Grey Lady* reputedly haunts the castle. Aldourie dates from the 17th century when it was held by the Frasers, but was rebuilt and extended in 1853.

4 Ardblair Castle

Off A923, 1 mile W of Blairgowrie, Perthshire
NO 164445   OS: 53

Ardblair Castle reputedly has a *Green Lady*, dressed in green silk, Lady Jean Drummond of nearby Newton Castle, which she is also said to haunt. She had fallen in love with one of the Blairs of Ardblair, but the two families feuded and the romance was doomed. In 1554 the Blair family was tried for the murder of George Drummond of Ledcrieff and his son, and Patrick Blair of Ardblair was beheaded. Lady Jean seems to have languished with a broken heart, and was drowned in a nearby marsh. However, her ghost reputedly searches through both castles, silently opening doors and passing down corridors, and is said to have been seen in recent times.

   The castle may date from as early as the 14th century, when the property was acquired by the Blairs, and consists of an L-plan tower and later wing with a courtyard. In 1792 the castle passed to the Oliphants of Gask, whose descendants still live here.

5 Ardrossan Castle

Off A78, in Ardrossan, Ayrshire
NS 233424   OS: 63

Not much remains of Ardrossan Castle, standing on a ridge called Castle Hill, above the town and harbour. In the 13th century, during the Wars of Independence, William Wallace captured the castle from the English. He

had the garrison slaughtered and thrown into the dungeon, the event afterwards known as *Wallace's Larder*. Wallace was eventually captured, and hanged, drawn and quartered in London in 1305. His ghost can reputedly be seen here on stormy nights.

The castle was acquired by Sir John Montgomery who fought at the Battle of Otterburn in 1388, and captured Harry *Hotspur* Percy. It was little used by the 17th century, and much of the stone was carried off by Cromwell to build a fort at Ayr. The ruin is in a dangerous condition, although it is haunted by more than William Wallace if all the empty drinks bottles and cans are anything to go by.

Open all year – ruin in a dangerous condition

6 Ardvreck Castle

Off A837, 1.5 miles NW of Inchnadamph, Sutherland
NC 240236 OS: 15

The ruined MacLeod castle of Ardvreck consists of a keep and round tower with a square caphouse.

It was here, in 1650, that James Graham, Marquis of Montrose, was betrayed to the Covenanters after losing the Battle of Carbisdale. He was taken to Edinburgh and executed, his body dismembered and displayed in public.

Much evil and dabbling with the devil are linked with the castle. The

13

distraught ghost of one of the daughters of a MacLeod chief is said to haunt the ruins. She was apparently betrothed to the devil as reward for his help in building the castle, but threw herself out of one of the windows rather than marry. Another spectre associated with the castle is that of a tall grey-clothed man.

7 Ashintully Castle

Off B950, 2 miles NE of Kirkmichael, Perthshire
NO 101613   OS: 43

Ashintully, a 16th-century tower house built by the Spaldings, is said to be haunted by the ghost of *Green Jean*. She inherited the castle and lands in her own right, but her uncle wanted the property. In one of the castle chambers, he murdered Jean – who was wearing a green dress – and her servant, who he stuffed up the chimney. Jean's ghost is said to be seen at the family burial ground, beside her memorial, and her footsteps have been heard in the castle.

Two other ghosts are also said to haunt the grounds: one a messenger, who was wrongly murdered for not having delivered a message; the other a tinker who was hanged for trespassing and cursed the family.

8 Auchinvole House

Off B802 or B8023, 0.5 miles S of Kilsyth, Lanarkshire
NS 714769   OS: 64

Auchinvole House, an altered 16th-century tower house of the Stark family, is said to be haunted by a female ghost. Sitting at one of the castle windows, the spirit reputedly gazes to where her murdered lover was buried.

9 Balcomie Castle

Off A917, 1.5 miles NE of Crail, Fife
NO 626099   OS: 59

The lands of Balcomie were held by a John de Balcomie in 1375, although the existing castle, with turrets and stair-tower, dates from no earlier than the 16th century. The spirit of a young man, who was starved to death here, is said to manifest itself by whistling.

10 Baldoon Castle

Off A746, 1.5 miles S of Wigtown, Dumfries & Galloway
NX 426536   OS: 83

Janet Dalrymple of Carscreugh was forced to marry Sir David Dunbar of Baldoon Castle in 1669. She loved another man, Archibald Rutherford, but he was poor and her parents insisted that she married Dunbar. Janet died soon after the marriage, either murdered on her wedding night or dying insane soon afterwards. Her husband, however, went on to marry a daughter of the Montgomery Earl of Eglinton. Janet's ghost, in a bloodied wedding dress, is said to haunt the ruined remains of the castle on the anniversary of her death, 12 September.

11 Balgonie Castle

Off A911, 3.5 miles E of Glenrothes, Fife
NO 313007   OS: 59

Balgonie Castle is a fine 14th-century castle with a courtyard enclosing ranges of buildings, some of them ruined. It was built by the Sibbalds, who held the property from before 1246, but passed by marriage to Sir Robert Lundie, later Lord High Treasurer, who extended the castle about 1496. James IV visited the castle the same year, as did Mary, Queen of Scots, in 1565. The castle was captured and sacked by Rob Roy MacGregor in 1716.

One range is haunted by a *Green Lady,* thought to be the spirit of one of the Lundies. Her ghost has been seen in recent times on the stair of the castle, and is recorded in 1842 as being a well-known ghost.

The apparition of a 17th-century soldier has been witnessed in the courtyard, while the most haunted part of the castle is the hall, and apparitions and ghostly voices have been heard here.

☎ 01592 750119—Open all year – available for weddings and other functions

  ⅃ ♿ Access to ground floor only

12 Ballindalloch Castle

Off A95, 7.5 miles SW of Charlestown of Aberlour

NJ 178365 OS: 28

Situated in pleasant gardens and grounds, Ballindalloch Castle incorporates a 16th-century Z-plan tower house, and was extended and altered in the 18th century and again in 1845. The castle was sacked

during a feud with the Gordons, and was burned by the Marquis of Montrose in 1645. The lands were held by the Grants by 1499, but in the 18th century passed by marriage to the Macphersons, and descendants of the family still live here.

The castle is said to be haunted by a *Green Lady*, who frequents the old hall, which is now used as the dining room. Two other ghosts are also associated with Ballindalloch, one reputed to be the spirit of General James Grant, who died in 1806. Mounted on a horse, the ghost of Grant is said ride around and review the estate – of which has was very proud in life – every night. He is then said to go to the wine-cellar. Another ghost is that of a girl – a jilted lover – who is supposed to have been seen at the nearby Bridge of Avon.

☎ 01807 500206—Open Easter to end September

13 Balmoral Castle

Off B976, 7 miles W of Ballater, Aberdeenshire
Of B976 just south of junction with A93, at Balmoral,
Aberdeenshire.

NO 255952   OS: 44

Although there was an older stronghold on the site, Balmoral Castle
dates from 1855, and was the holiday home of Queen Victoria and Prince
Albert. It is still used by the present Royal family. Exhibition of paintings
in ballroom and grounds only.

John Brown, a manservant to Queen Victoria, is said to haunt the castle.

☎ 01339 742471—Open May to July

 &

14 Balnagown Castle

Off A9, 8 miles NE of Alness, Highland
NH 763752   OS: 21

Balnagown was built by the Ross family about 1375, and remained with
the family until 1978. The old part consists of a main block with two
towers, and was much altered and added to in later centuries

Although the Ross family were as lawless as most – the 8th laird,
Alexander, terrorised the area until imprisoned; his son, George, was
little better; and his daughter, Katherine, was accused of witchcraft – it is
a Munro who is said to haunt the castle. *Black* Andrew Munro – a man of
many dark deeds, especially in dealing with women – was hanged for his
crimes from one of the windows. His ghost is said to haunt the castle,
and mostly appears to women. A *Grey Lady*, the ghost of a young woman
clad in a grey dress – a murdered 'Scottish princess' – has also reportedly
been seen. Both ghosts are said to have apparently been witnessed in the
20th century.

15 Barcaldine Castle

Off A828, 4 miles N of Connel, Argyll
NM 907405   OS: 49

Formerly known as the Black Castle of Barcaldine, Barcaldine was built by
Sir Duncan Campbell of Glenorchy – *Black Duncan of the Castles* – who
also built strongholds at Kilchurn, Achallader, Loch Dochart, Finlarig,

Balloch – now called Taymouth – and Edinample. It is a fine tower house with a round stair-tower and angle-turrets; and has a heavy iron yett behind an oak door. The castle had become ruinous by the 19th century, but has been restored and is occupied.

In 1752, the Barcaldine Campbells were involved in the plot to murder the *Red Fox*, Sir Colin Campbell of Glenure. The murder is recounted in Robert Louis Stevenson's *Kidnapped*. The spectres of the Campbell of Glenure reputedly haunts the castle, as does a *Blue Lady*.

16 Barnbougle Castle

Off A924, 2.5 miles E of South Queensferry, West Lothian
NT 169785 OS: 65

Barnbougle Castle, mostly dating from 1881, incorporates some work from a stronghold of the 16th century. It was held by the Mowbrays of Barnbougle from the 12th century, and it is during their ownership – at the time of the Crusades – that the ghost story originates. A hound is said to haunt the grounds of Barnbougle, and howl shortly before the Laird of Barnbougle is to die. This is reputedly the origin of the name of *Hound Point*, just to the north-west of Barnbougle, and now a tanker berth.

Barnbougle passed in 1662 to the Primrose family – Archibald Philip Primrose was Prime Minister between 1894-5.

17 Bedlay Castle

Off A80, 3 miles SE of Kirkintilloch, Lanarkshire
NS 692701 OS: 64

Bedlay Castle is said to be haunted by the ghost of Bishop Cameron, who died in suspicious circumstances about 1350. Hauntings in the house, including an apparition of a large bearded man, were recorded in the 1970s. The castle, however, was built by the Boyds of Kilmarnock – who acquired the lands at the Reformation in the 16th century – although it may incorporate an older stronghold.

18 The Binns

Off A904, 3 miles E of Linlithgow, West Lothian
NTS NT 051785 OS: 65

The Binns, a mansion of about 1800, incorporates part of a 15th-century castle, and has some fine plaster ceilings from the early 17th century. The

Binns was presented to the National Trust for Scotland in 1944, and there is a park around the house.

It was a property of William Dalziel of The Binns. He was taken prisoner in 1651 at the Battle of Worcester, when in the army of Charles II which was defeated by Cromwell – but escaped from the Tower of London. Going into exile, he served in the Russian army with the Tsar's cossacks. He returned after the Restoration, and was made commander of forces in Scotland from 1666 to 1685. He led the force that defeated the Covenanters at the Battle of Rullion Green in 1666, and the Cameronians at the Battle of Airds Moss in 1680. He died in 1685, and the house and grounds are reputedly haunted by his ghost, which is sometimes seen on a white horse riding up to the door. One story is that Dalziel often played cards with the devil, and once when he won the devil was so enraged that it threw a massive marble table, on which they had been playing, into a nearby pond. When the water was low after a drought, this table was supposedly found over 200 years after Dalziel's death. Another ghost, said to haunt the grounds, is that of an old man gathering firewood.

☏ 01506 834255—Open May to September except closed Fri; grounds open all year

19 Borthwick Castle

Off A7, 2 miles SE of Gorebridge, Midlothian
NT 370597   OS: 66
One of the most magnificent and daunting castles in Scotland, Borthwick Castle is a massive U-plan keep with thick walls and a stone flagged roof. The fine vaulted hall, on the first floor, has a minstrels' gallery reached by a small stair. Building began in 1420 by the Borthwick family, and the castle formerly had a curtain wall

and corner towers.

James Hepburn, the Earl of Bothwell, and Mary, Queen of Scots, visited the castle in 1567 after their wedding, but were besieged here, Mary only escaping disguised as a page boy. The castle was abandoned in the 17th century, but restored in 1890.

Ann Grant, a young peasant girl – who had been made pregnant by one of the Borthwick lords – is said to have been murdered, and her remains concealed within the castle. The *Red Room* in the castle is reputed to be haunted by her spirit.

☎ 01875 820514—Hotel – open mid-March to January 2 and to non-residents

20 Braco Castle

Braco, Perth & Kinross, Tayside
Of B8033, 6 miles N of Dunblane, Perthshire.
NN 824113   OS: 57
Braco was a property of the Graham Earls of Montrose, who built a tower house here in the 16th century. The castle was extended in later centuries, and is said to be haunted.

21 Braemar Castle

Off A93, 0.5 miles NE of
Braemar, Aberdeenshire
NO 156924   OS: 43
Braemar Castle is an
interesting tower house, with
battlemented corner turrets,
which was built about 1628
by the Earl of Mar. The 1715
Jacobite Rising was led by
John Erskine, Earl of Mar,
and his forces were
marshalled here. The castle is
still occupied, and there are
many interesting rooms.

The ghost of a fair young
woman is said to haunt the

castle. A bride, wrongly believing herself abandoned by her new husband, is said to have committed suicide within the walls. A sighting of the apparition was reported in 1987. Another spirit is supposedly that of John Farquharson of Inverey, also known as the *Black Colonel*, who summoned servants by firing a pistol.

☎ 01339 741224—Open Easter to end October

🅿 S 🆆🅲 ♿

22 Brahan Castle

Off A835, 3.5 miles SW of Dingwall, Highland

Ruin or site   NH 513549   26

Brahan was a castle and mansion of the Mackenzie Earls of Seaforth, but was completely demolished in the 1950s. The family lost everything as foretold by the Brahan Seer, Kenneth Mackenzie. Isabella, 3rd Countess of Seaforth, demanded to know why her husband remained in Paris. Furious when she was told that her husband had taken up with a French lady, she decided to *shoot the messenger* and ordered Kenneth to be burnt in a barrel of tar. Before he died, Kenneth predicted that the last chief would follow his sons to the grave, deaf and dumb, and that one of his daughters would kill the other. The last chief became deaf through illness – and then finally too weak to speak– but only died after seeing his four sons predecease him. The carriage his eldest daughter was driving accidentally overturned and killed her sister.

A nearby stretch of the Conon River is said to have a water sprite.

23 Brodick Castle

Off A841, 1.5 miles N of Brodick, Arran, Ayrshire

NTS   NS 016378   69

In wooded grounds and with a fine walled garden, Brodick Castle dates partly from the 13th and 15th centuries – although it was greatly extended and remodelled in the 19th century. The old part rises to three storeys and has a crenellated parapet.

The castle was garrisoned for the English during the Wars of Independence until recaptured by the Scots in 1307. The Hamiltons acquired the property and held it until 1958, when it was acquired by the National Trust for Scotland.

A *Grey Lady* is said to have been seen in the older part, possibly a plague

victim left to die in the dungeons. The spectre of a sitting man has apparently been seen in the library; and a White Deer is said to appear when one of the chiefs of the Hamiltons dies.

☎ 01770 302202—Castle open April to October; garden and country park open all year

P ☕ S wc ₤ ♿ Facilities

24 Buchanan Castle

Off B807, 0.5 miles W of Drymen, Stirlingshire
NS 463886 OS: 57

The original castle – which was burnt down in 1850 and replaced by a huge baronial house, itself now a ruin – was held by the Buchanans, and then the Grahams. The house is said to be haunted. Rudolf Hess, Hitler's deputy, was imprisoned here after flying to Scotland.

25 Buckholm Tower

Off A7, 1 mile N of Galashiels, Borders
NT 482379 OS: 73

Buckholm Tower is a ruined 16th-century tower house, which was built by the Pringles. They were accused of treason and their tower was burnt in 1547. It was restored, but is now derelict.

One story is that the ruins are haunted by one of the 17th-century Pringle lairds. He was a cruel man, spending his time persecuting Covenanters and murdering folk in his dungeon. He was cursed by the wife of one of his victims, and afterwards lived in great terror, as if pursued by ghostly hounds. Pringle's ghost can reputedly be seen running from howling dogs on the anniversary of his death, and screams and cries heard emanating from the dungeon.

26 Carleton Castle

Off A77, 6 miles S of Girvan, Ayrshire
NX 133895   OS: 76

The ghost of Sir John Cathcart is said to haunt the ruins of the 15th-century castle. Cathcart murdered several of his wives, and secretly disposed of their remains. However, his last wife, May Kennedy of Culzean, realising what was to happen to her, managed to save herself by pushing Cathcart to his death off nearby cliffs. It is said that ghostly cries and screams have been heard from within the crumbling castle walls.

27 Caroline Park House

Granton, Midlothian & Edinburgh, Lothian
Off A901, 3 miles N of Edinburgh Castle
NT 227773   OS: 66

A *Green Lady* – believed to be the spirit of Lady Royston, wife of Sir James Mackenzie of Tarbat – is said to haunt Caroline Park, part of which dates from about 1585. Her spirit rises from an old well and drifts over to the entrance of the house. A ghostly cannon ball has reputedly been witnessed several times, smashing through a window of one chamber and rolling along the floor, although it does no apparent damage.

28 Castle Cary

Off A80, 2 miles NE of Cumbernauld, Falkirk
NS 786775   64

Castle Cary consists of a 15th-century keep, with a crenellated parapet, to which has been added 17th-century extensions. Two ghosts are said to have been witnessed in the building. One is William Baillie of Letham, whose family held the property from the 17th century after it had passed from the Livingstones. Baillie was the general of Covenanter forces who was defeated at the battles of Kilsyth and Alford in 1645 by the Marquis of Montrose. The other spirit is reputedly Lizzie Baillie, his daughter. Lizzie eloped with a poor farmer, and the news is said to have killed her father – she looks through the castle's chambers, searching for Baillie.

29 Castle Coeffin

Off B8045, 8.5 miles N of Oban, west coast of island of Lismore, Argyll

NM 853437 OS: 49

Standing on a rock, Castle Coeffin is a fragmentary and overgrown ruin, once held by the MacDougalls of Lorn, and dating mostly from around the 13th century.

   The ghost story, however, dates from long before this. The stronghold is said to be named after Caifen, son of a Norse king, who lived here. His sister, Beothail, died of a broken heart after her lover was slain in Norway. Her ghost then began to haunt the castle, and did not find peace until she was taken to Norway and buried beside her lover.

30 Castle Fraser

Off B993 or B977, 6.5 miles SW of Inverurie, Aberdeenshire

NTS NJ 724126 38

Impressive and well preserved, Castle Fraser is a tall and massive castle, dating in part from the 15th century. The property was acquired by the Frasers in 1454. The family were Jacobites, and the 4th Lord died a fugitive, falling from a cliff, after the 1715 Rising. In 1976 the property was donated to the National Trust for Scotland, and there is a garden.

   A young woman is said to have been murdered in the castle in the 19th century, her body dragged down stairs before being buried. The blood, which stained the steps, could not be cleaned off – or so the story goes.

📞 01330 833463—Castle open Easter weekend; May to September; weekends only in October; garden open all year

P ☕ **S** 📶 £ ♿ Facilities

31 Castle Grant

Off A939, 1.5 miles N of Grantown-on-Spey, Highland

NJ 041302 36

Lady Barbara Grant, daughter of a 16th-century laird, was imprisoned in a dark closet in the castle when she fell in love with a man her father

considered unsuitable. She died heartbroken, and her ghost is said to appear from behind tapestries – concealing the closet – and flit across the bedroom. The apparition has also reportedly been seen washing her hands in another of the bedrooms.

The castle, dating from the 15th century but greatly altered and extended in following centuries, belonged to the Grants, and became their chief stronghold. The Grants were Hanoverians and fought against the Jacobites in both the 1715 and 1745 Risings.

32 Castle Levan

Off A770, 1.5 miles SW of Gourock, Renfrewshire

NS 216764 OS: 63

Standing on at the edge of a ravine, Castle Levan consists of a 14th-century keep and offset 16th-century tower. It was built by the Mortons, but is reputedly haunted by a *White Lady*, ghost of Lady Montgomery, who was starved to death by her husband for mistreating local tenants and farmers.

33 Castle Stuart

Off A96, 6 miles NE of Inverness, Highland

NH 742498   OS: 27

Castle Stuart is an impressive 17th-century tower house, crowned with angle-turrets, one of which is said to be haunted. It may incorporate work from the 14th century, when it was held by the Mackintoshes, although it later passed to the Earls of Moray.

34 Castle of Mey

Off A836, 7 miles NE of Castletown, Caithness

ND 290739   OS: 12

The Castle of Mey, owned by the Her Majesty Queen Elizabeth, the Queen Mother, is an altered tower house, dating from the 16th century – although it was extended in later centuries. The first castle was built by the Earl of Caithness, and is said to be haunted by the ghost of a daughter of the 5th Earl. She fell in love with a ploughman, and her disapproving father had her imprisoned in one of the attic rooms. In despair, the poor girl threw herself from one of the windows, and was killed in the fall. Her sad apparition, the *Green Lady* , has reputedly been seen in the castle.

The gardens are occasionally open

35 Castle of Moy

Off A849, 10 miles SW of Craignure, Mull, Argyll

NM 616247   OS: 49

In a beautiful situation on a rocky crag by the seashore, the Castle of Moy, at Lochbuie, is a stark ruinous keep, complete to the parapet. The castle had been abandoned by 1752, but the MacLaines, an unruly branch of the MacLeans, owned the property until the 20th century.

In earlier centuries, father – Iain the Toothless – and his son and heir – Ewen of the Little Head – feuded over a marriage settlement, and Ewan was slain and beheaded in the subsequent battle, his horse riding off with his corpse. His ghost, the headless horseman, is still said to ride along Glen Mor, appearing when one of the family is about to die.

MacLean of Duart, seeing a chance to gain the lands, captured Iain the

Toothless, and confined him in the castle of Cairnburg, on one of the Treshnish Isles, to prevent him producing an new heir. Iain's only female companion was reputedly a deformed and ugly woman, but he still contrived to make her pregnant. MacLaine himself was murdered soon afterwards, but the woman managed to escape and produced a son – Murdoch the Stunted – who eventually regained the castle and lands.

Open all year — view from exterior

36 Castle of Park

Off A75, 0.5 miles W of Glenluce village, Dumfries & Galloway
NX 189571   OS: 82

The Hays built the tower house, with its steeply pitched roof, in 1590, and the building was restored in recent times. It is reputed to be haunted by the ghost of a monk, who was walled up in one of the rooms. A *Green Lady* is also said to haunt the castle. Becoming pregnant while working at the house, the poor girl then hanged herself. Both ghosts are said to have been seen in recent times.

37 Cawdor Castle

Cawdor, Inverness & Nairn, Highland
Off B9090, 5 miles SW of Nairn, Nairn
NH 847499   OS: 27

One of the most magnificent and well preserved strongholds in Scotland, Cawdor Castle incorporates a 14th-century keep – built around a holly tree – surrounded by a courtyard with a ditch and reached by a drawbridge. There are many portraits, furnishings, a collection of tapestries, and fine flower gardens.

The title *Thane of Cawdor* is associated with Macbeth, but if the murder of Duncan took place, it was not at the present castle. The Campbells obtained Cawdor by kidnapping the girl heiress, Muriel Calder, in 1511 and marrying her to the Earl of Argyll's son, Sir John Campbell.

The castle is reputedly haunted by the handless ghost of a beautiful young woman, who is said – in life – to have fallen in love with the son of a laird from a rival family. The two families were bitter foes, and when her father found out, he pursued her through the castle, until he caught her in one of the upper chambers and cut her hands off. She then fell to her death from the tower, and since then her ghost is said to haunt Cawdor.

☎ 01667 404615—Open 1 May to 12 October

38 Cessnock Castle

Off B7037, 1 mile SE of Galston, Ayrshire
NS 511355   OS: 70

Standing above a ravine, Cessnock Castle, built by the Campbells, is a massive keep, dating from the 15th century, to which has been added a large mansion. The great hall has a late 16th-century painted ceiling.

Mary, Queen of Scots, came to Cessnock after her defeat at the Battle of Langside in 1568. One of her ladies died here, and is said to haunt the castle. John Knox also visited and his apparition is also said to have been seen within the walls – quoting scriptures – although the two spirits may make uncomfortable companions.

39 Claypotts Castle

Off A92, 3.5 miles E of Dundee city centre
His Scot   NO 452319   OS: 54

An unusual and impressive tower house, Claypotts Castle consists of a rectangular main block and two large round towers at opposite corners. In the 17th century, the castle was held by John Graham of Claverhouse, Viscount Dundee, who was known as *Bloody Clavers* – for his cruel persecution of Covenanters – as well as *Bonnie Dundee* – after his death in 1689 at the victory over the forces of William and Mary at the Battle of Killiecrankie. However, the haunting dates from around the building of the castle. A *White Lady*, thought to be the ghost of Marion Ogilvie, mistress of Cardinal David Beaton, is said to have been seen here. Beaton was murdered at St Andrews Castle in 1546.

Open all year – view from exterior only

Nearby

40 Cloncaird Castle

Off B7045, 4 miles E of Maybole, Ayrshire
NS 359075   OS: 70

Cloncaird Castle, a 16th-century tower house, was built by the Mure family. It was much extended and remodelled in the Gothic style in 1841, and is still occupied. An apparition of a man is said to have been seen on the stairs, even in recent times.

41 Comlongon Castle

Off B724, 8 miles SE of Dumfries
NY 079690   OS: 85

Comlongon Castle is a massive 15th-century castle, built by the Murrays of Cockpool, who became Earls of Annandale, and later Earls of Mansfield. A large 19th-century mansion stands nearby.

The castle is said to be haunted by a *Green Lady*, believed to be spirit of Marion Carruthers. She was forced into a betrothal of marriage with a man she did not love, and fled to Comlongon after escaping from imprisonment in Hermitage Castle. She committed suicide at Comlongon rather than wed, and reputedly haunts the castle.

42 Corgarff Castle

Off A939, 12 miles NW of Ballater, Aberdeenshire
His Scot   NJ 255086
OS: 37

Corgarff Castle consists of a much-altered 16th-century tower house, surrounded by later star-shaped artillery emplacements. The castle was burnt out in 1571, killing Margaret Campbell – wife of Forbes of Towie – and 26 others of her household. Adam Gordon of Auchindoun was responsible for the slaughter – supposedly in support of Mary, Queen of Scots – the story recounted in the ballad *Edom o' Gordon*. Ghostly screams are said to have been heard here, and may originate from this event. Corgarff saw action during the Jacobite Risings, was later used as a base to help stop illicit whisky distilling. A recreated barrack room, from this period, is housed in the castle.

☎ 01975 651460—Open daily April to September; weekends only October to March – involves short walk

43 Coroghon Castle

On E end of island of Canna, Highland

NG 288055 39

Not much remains of a castle on the summit of a steep rock. The site is said to be haunted by the ghost of a woman imprisoned here by one of the MacDonald Lord of the Isles.

44 Corstorphine Castle

Off A8, 3 miles W of Edinburgh Castle

NT 203730 OS: 66

Nothing remains of the stronghold here, owned by the Forresters, which was occupied until at least 1698, although some remains survived to at least 1870. The grounds around the site are still said to be haunted by a *White Lady*, throught to be the ghost of a Christian Nimmo. She murdered her lover – one of the Forresters of Corstorphine – in 1679 during an argument. Tried for the murdered and sentenced to death, she briefly managed to escape, only to be recaptured and executed.

45 Cortachy Castle

Off B955, 3.5 miles N of Kirriemuir, Angus

NO 398597 54

Cortachy Castle is said to be haunted by a ghostly drummer, who can be heard drumming whenever one of the Ogilvies nears death. The ghost is thought to be the spirit of a drummer from the Leslie family, who angered the family and was slain, either by burning or by being thrown from the battlements. It is said that the drums were heard several times in the 19th century, and heralded deaths in the family.

Cortachy, an extended 15th-century courtyard castle, was built by the Ogilvie Earls of Airlie. Charles II spent a night at Cortachy in 1650 in the *King's Room*, and the following year the castle was sacked by Cromwell in reprisal.

46 Craigcrook Castle

Off A90, 2.5 miles W of Edinburgh Castle
NT 211742   OS: 66

Craigcrook, a modified and extended 16th-century tower house, was probably built by the Adamson family, and is reputedly haunted.

47 Craigievar Castle

Off A980, 4.5 miles S of Alford, Aberdeenshire
NTS   NJ 566095   OS: 37

A well-preserved and picturesque castle, Craigievar is a massive tower house with a profusion of turrets, gables, chimney-stacks and corbelling crowning the upper storeys, while the lower part of the walls are plain. The hall has a fine large fireplace, with an ornamental stone carving.

The castle was started by the Mortimer family, but they ran out of money, and it was sold to the Forbeses, who finished building in 1626. The castle passed to the National Trust for Scotland in 1963.

Craigievar is said to be haunted by an apparition, thought to be one of the Gordon family, who was murdered by being pushed from one of the upper windows.

48 Craignethan Castle

Off A72, 4.5 miles W of Lanark, Lanarkshire
His Scot   NS 816464   OS: 72

Standing on a promontory above a deep ravine, Craignethan consists a strong tower, once surrounded by a curtain wall and corner towers, with a massively thick rampart protecting the landward side. It was built to withstand artillery, and has a deep ditch with a caponier. There is a small exhibition.

The castle was built by the Hamiltons, who supported Mary, Queen of Scots. Mary is said to have spent the night here before the Battle of Langside in 1568. The Hamiltons formed the main part of her army, but

were defeated by the Regent Moray, and Mary fled to England. Sir Walter Scott featured Craignethan in *Old Mortality*, but called it Tillietudlem. It passed into the care of the state in 1949.

The castle is said to be haunted by a headless ghost, perhaps the spirit of Mary, Queen of Scots – although this seems unlikely as her association with Craignethan is limited to one visit at most – as well as by other ghosts in the later house in the outer courtyard.

☎ 01555 860364—Open daily March to October except Thur PM and Fri

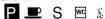

49 Cranshaws

Off B6355, 0.5 miles W of Cranshaws, Borders

NT 681619   OS: 67

Cranshaws, a tower house built by the Douglases, dates partly from the 15th century. The castle is supposed to have had a brownie, a supernatural sprite, which did all manner of chores. Having gathered and threshed the corn for a number of years, one of the servants complained that it was not done very neatly. The next day the grain was found two miles away in the Whiteadder river – it was better to look after such spirits, and they were normally given gifts, such as food and drink.

50 Crathes Castle

Off A93, 2 miles E of Banchory, Aberdeenshire

NTS NO 734968 45

One of the finest surviving castles in Scotland, Crathes Castle is a massive 16th-century tower house. The upper storeys are adorned with much corbelling, angle and stair-turrets, and decoration; while the lower storeys are very plain. There are many fine tempera and plaster ceilings, a splendid garden, and a visitor centre.

The property was owned by the Burnetts of Leys from the 14th century, their original castle being in the now drained Loch of Leys. The jewelled

ivory *Horn of Leys* is kept at Crathes, and was given to the Burnetts in 1323 by Robert the Bruce. Around 1553, the Burnetts began to build the new castle at Crathes, but it was not completed until 1596. It passed to the National Trust for Scotland in 1951.

One of the chambers, the *Green Lady's* room, is said to be haunted by a ghost which has been seen many times. The ghost first appeared in the 18th century, and is seen crossing the chamber, with a baby in her arms, to disappear at the fire-place. The young woman seems to have been a daughter of the then laird, and had been dallying with a servant. It appears that she was murdered to hide her pregnancy. The skeletons of a young woman and baby were found by workmen under the hearthstone.

☎ 01330 844525—Open April to October; grounds and gardens open all year

P ☕ **S** 🚾 ⚲ ♿ 🚾/Access to castle ground floor

51 Crichton Castle

Off B6367, 2 miles E of Gorebridge, Midlothian

His Scot   NT 380612   OS: 66

A complex and interesting building, Crichton Castle consists of ranges of buildings from the 14th to 16th centuries, enclosing a small courtyard. A notable feature is an arcaded, diamond-faced facade within the courtyard.

The castle was built by the Crichtons. Sir William Crichton, Chancellor of Scotland, entertained the young Earl of Douglas and his brother in 1440 here before having them murdered at the *Black Dinner* in Edinburgh Castle. The property passed to the Hepburns. One of the family was Patrick Hepburn, Earl of Bothwell, third husband of Mary, Queen of Scots – Mary attended a wedding here in 1562. Turner painted the castle, and Walter Scott included it in *Marmion*.

The castle is said to be haunted by a horseman, who enters the castle by the original gate, which is now walled up. Outside the castle are the roofless stables, reputedly haunted by the ghost of William Crichton.

☎ 01875 320017—Open April to September – 600 yard walk

 P S 𝄞

52 Cromarty Castle

Off A832, 0.5 miles SE of Cromarty, Highland

NH 794670   OS: 27

Nothing remains of Cromarty Castle, built by the Urquharts, which partly dated from the 12th century. The castle, which was said to be haunted, was demolished in 1772; and Cromarty House, an imposing classical mansion, was built on the site.

53 Culcreuch Castle

Culcreuch, Stirling, Central

Off B822, 0.5 miles N of Fintry, Stirlingshire

NS 620876   OS: 57

Culcreuch Castle, consisting of an altered 15th-century keep and extended in the 18th century, was probably built by the Galbraiths. The castle is said to be haunted by a ghostly piper, and there have reputedly been other manifestations within the walls.

☎ 01132 860228—Hotel – open all year and to non-residents

54 Cullen House

Off A98, 0 .5 miles SW of Cullen, Aberdeenshire

NJ 507663   OS: 29

Situated on a strong site above a deep ravine, Cullen House incorporates an altered 16th-century tower house of the Ogilvie Earls of Findlater. In 1645 the house was plundered by Royalists under the Marquis of Montrose. The house was converted into flats in the 1980s.

It is said that the ghost of the 3rd Earl of Findlater haunts the castle. Although in good health most of the time, he suffered from periods of uncontrollable madness, and during one such episode in 1770 murdered his factor, and later killed himself. His apparition was said to have been seen in 1943, and ghostly footsteps have reportedly often been heard, including by a band of Fleet Street journalists in 1964.

55 Culloden House

Off A96, 3.5 miles E of Inverness, Highland

NH 721465   OS: 27

Culloden House, dating mostly from 1772-83, incorporates the cellars of a 17th-century tower house. It was a property of the Forbes family, but the old tower was destroyed by the Duke of Cumberland in 1746 after the Battle of Culloden. The house has many Jacobite mementoes, and is now used as a hotel. One story is that the house is haunted by the ghost of Bonnie Prince Charlie, although this is disputed.

✆ 01463 790461—Hotel – open all year and to non-residents

56 Culzean Castle

Off A77, 4.5 miles W of Maybole, Ayrshire

NTS   NS 233103   OS: 70

Culzean Castle, built between 1777-92 and designed by Robert Adam, incorporates part of a 16th-century tower house, which itself was built on the site of an older castle. In 1601 the castle was a property of the Kennedys. Thomas Kennedy of Culzean was slain by the Mure Lord Auchendrane during a feud started by the cold-blooded murder of Kennedy of Bargany. In 1945 Culzean passed to the National Trust for Scotland, and is now one of the foremost tourist attractions in Scotland.

A ghostly piper is said to herald when one of the Kennedys is about to get married, and plays on stormy nights. His apparition has been seen in

the grounds. There are said to be two other ghosts, one a young woman dressed in a ball gown. Sightings of a ghost were reported in 1972.

📞 01655 760274—Open April to October; park open all year

 Facilities

57 Dean Castle

Off B7038, 1 mile NE of Kilmarnock, Ayrshire
NS 437394 OS: 70

Interesting and well preserved, Dean Castle consists of a 14th-century keep, with a crenellated parapet, and a 15th-century palace block, enclosed within a courtyard. The castle was restored from 1905, and now houses a museum, containing a collection of armour and musical instruments, and is surrounded by a public park.

  The castle was started by the Boyds, later Earls of Kilmarnock, about 1460, although it may incorporate earlier work. Robert Boyd became Guardian of James III, and practically ruled Scotland from 1466-69. The 4th Earl, William Boyd, was Privy Councillor to Bonnie Prince Charlie during the Jacobite Rising of 1745. However, before he joined the Rising, his servants were terrified by an apparition of his severed head rolling about the floor. Boyd was a Colonel in the Prince's guard, but was captured after the Battle of Culloden in 1746, and was beheaded.

📞 01563 526401—Castle open from 12 noon all year

P ☕ S 🚾 ⚿ ♿ Limited access

58 Delgatie Castle

Off A947, 2 miles E of Delgatie, Aberdeenshire
NJ 755506   OS: 29

An imposing and well-preserved building, Delgatie Castle consists of an altered and extended keep, dating from the 15th century, although it may incorporate older work.

Delgatie was a property of the Hays, who were created Earls of Errol in 1452. Mary, Queen of Scots, spent three days here after the Battle of Corrichie in 1562. The 9th Earl was summoned for treason in 1594 for supporting the Gordon Earl of Huntly, and part of the west wall was battered down by James VI's forces. Sir William Hay of Delgatie was Standard Bearer to the Marquis of Montrose during his campaign of 1645. Although defeated at the Battle of Philiphaugh, Hay managed to return the Standard to Buchanan Castle, but he was executed with Montrose at Edinburgh in 1650, and buried beside him in St Giles Cathedral. The castle is now the private home of Captain John Hay of Delgatie, and was made the Clan Hay centre in 1948.

The apparition of a red-haired young woman is said to have been seen in the castle.

☎ 01888 563479—Open April to October

🅿 ☕ S 🚻 ⅋ ♿ 🚾/Access to ground floor and tea-room

59 Drumlanrig Castle

Off A6, 3 miles NW of Thornhill, Dumfries & Galloway
NX 851992   OS: 78

The large imposing symmetrical mansion, started in the 18th century, incorporates cellers from a 14th-century castle of the Douglases. Mary, Queen of Scots, stayed here in 1563. The house is still occupied, and has a fine collection of pictures, including works by Rembrandt, Holbein and Leonardo. There is a garden and visitor centre.

Three ghosts are said to haunt Drumlanrig. One is reputed to be the spirit of Lady Anne Douglas; another that of a young woman in a flowing dress; the third a monkey, or other similar creature.

☎ 01848 330248—Open early May to late August except Thur

🅿 ☕ S 🚻 ⅋ ♿ Access

60 Duart Castle

Off A849, 3 miles S of Craignure, Mull, Argyll

NM 749354 OS: 49

An extremely impressive and daunting fortress, Duart is a MacLean property, the family claiming descent from Gillean of the Blood Axe, an ancient hero. The castle, consisting of a strong curtain wall enclosing a massive keep and later ranges of buildings, was begun in the 13th century. In 1674, however, the property was acquired by the Campbell

Earl of Argyll, and Duart was abandoned after the Jacobite Rising of 1745 to become derelict and roofless. It was bought back by Fitzroy MacLean in 1911 – who restored the castle – and now houses a display of clan memorabilia.

In earlier times, the MacLeans of Duart feuded with a rival branch of the clan, the MacLaines of Lochbuie. Ewen of the Small head, a son of the Lochbuie branch – whose fortress was the Castle of Moy – was slain and beheaded; and his ghost, the headless horseman, is said still to ride through Glen Mor, heralding the death of one of the family.

One of the later MacLeans became so unhappy with his Campbell wife that in 1523 he had the poor woman chained to a rock in the Firth of Lorn to be drowned at high tide. However, she was rescued and taken to her father, the Campbell Earl of Argyll. As a result, MacLean was murdered in his bed at Edinburgh by one of her brothers.

☎ 01680 812309—Open May to mid-October

P 🍵 S 🚾 ⅃ ♿ Limited to access

61 Duchal Castle

Off B788, 1.5 miles W of Kilmacolm, Renfrewshire

NS 334685 OS: 63

Little remains of Duchal Castle, a 13th-century keep and courtyard of the Lyles, later made Lord High Justiciars of Scotland. The family took part in a rebellion of 1489, and James IV besieged Duchal, bringing with him the cannon *Mons Meg*, which survives at Edinburgh Castle. Later James visited the castle to see one of his mistresses, Marion Boyd. They had a son, who was made Archbishop of St Andrews, but was slain at the Battle of Flodden in 1513 with his father.

The castle was said to be haunted by the spirit of an excommunicated monk in the 13th century. The son of the house confronted and fought the evil ghost – and although the spirit of the monk was not seen again – the young man was slain.

62 Dunnottar Castle

Off A92, 2 miles S of Stonehaven, Aberdeenshire

NO 882839

OS: 45

Built on a high promontory, Dunnottar Castle is a spectacular ruined courtyard castle, parts of which date from the 12th century. Buildings include a 15th-century keep, 16th- and early 17th-century ranges, a large chapel, stable

block, forge, barracks and priest's house.

An early castle here was captured by William Wallace from the English in 1296. Edward III of England took the castle in the 1330s, but it was quickly recaptured for the Scots by Sir Andrew Moray, the Regent. The Keiths acquired the property in 1382, and by the beginning of the 16th century Dunnottar was one of the most powerful fortresses in Scotland. Mary, Queen of Scots, stayed here in 1562. The 9th Earl entertained King Charles II here in 1650, and in 1651 the Scottish crown jewels were brought here for safety during Cromwell's invasion of Scotland. General Lambert besieged the castle in 1652, but before the garrison surrendered, the Regalia was smuggled out to be hidden in nearby Kinneff Church. 167 Covenanters, both women and men, were packed into one of the vaulted cellars during a hot summer in 1687, and nine of them died – it is this chamber which is said to be haunted.

Getting to the castle involves a steep climb, and a steeper one back.

☎ 01569 762173—Open all year except weekends in winter, 25/26 December & 1/2 January

63 Dunphail Castle

Off A940, 6.5 miles S of Forres, Moray

NJ 007481 OS: 27

All that remains of Dunphail Castle, a 14th-century stronghold of the Comyns, is the vaulted basement.

Following a botched ambush of the Regent, the Comyns were besieged here by Andrew Moray, the Regent, in 1330, after they fleeing from Darnaway Castle. Moray could not take the castle, even after several days, until he managed to capture five of the garrison, including Alasdair Comyn of Dunphail, who had been out foraging for food to bring back to the starving garrison. Moray had the men executed, and their heads flung over the walls of the castle, reputedly crying *Here's beef for your bannocks*.

The last of the Comyn garrison tried to flee, but were slaughtered to a man by the Regent's men. In the 18th century, it is said that five skull-less skeletons were found buried near the castle. Headless ghosts are said to have been seen by the castle and within the walls, and tales of the sounds of fighting, screams and groans have also been recorded.

64 Dunrobin Castle

Off A9, 1.5 miles NE of Golspie, Sutherland

NC 852008 OS: 17

Dunrobin Castle consists of a 15th-century keep and later buildings, greatly enlarged in the 19th and 20th centuries into a *fairy-tale chateau*. There is a garden and museum.

The Sutherland family, created Earls of Sutherland in 1235, had a castle here in the 13th century, but it passed by marriage to the Gordons. At Helmsdale Castle, Isobel Sinclair poisoned John, 11th Earl of Sutherland, and his wife, hoping to secure the succession for her son, but the future

12th Earl escaped, and her own son was poisoned. The young Earl was eventually captured and forced to marry Barbara Sinclair – who was twice his age – by the Sinclair Earl of Caithness. When he came of age, he divorced her. The lands passed by marriage to the Marquis of Stafford in the 18th century. He was involved in the *Clearances*, burning cottages and turfing people out of their homes so that the land could be cleared for sheep. The castle was sold in 1984.

The upper floors of the castle are said to be haunted by the spectre of a daughter of the 14th Earl. She decided to elope with her lover, but her father – who considered the man unsuitable – found out and had her imprisoned in one of the attic rooms. She tried to escape by climbing down a rope from one of the windows, but her father surprised her, and she fell to her death. One of the rooms – where disturbances have reputedly been worst – has since been disused.

☎ 01408 633268—Open May to October

🅿 ☕ S 🆆 ♿

65 Duns Castle

Off A6112, 1 mile NW of Duns, Borders
NT 777544   OS: 67

Duns Castle incorporates a keep, said to have been built by Thomas Randolph, Earl of Moray, in 1320. The castle was later altered to L-plan, and then much altered and extended in the 18th and 19th centuries. It passed to the Hays of Drumelzier, and the ghost of Alexander Hay, who was killed at the Battle of Waterloo in 1815, is said to haunt the castle.

66 Dunstaffnage Castle

Off A85, 3.5 miles NE of Oban, Argyll
His Scot   NM 882344   OS: 49

A stronghold here was held by the kings of Dalriada in the 7th century, and was one of the places that the *Stone of Destiny* was kept. The present castle – a massive curtain wall, with round towers, and a later altered gatehouse – was begun by the MacDougalls in the 13th century. James IV twice visited at the end of the 15th century, and the Earl of Argyll burned the castle in 1685. Flora MacDonald was imprisoned here after helping Bonnie Prince Charlie escape from Hanoverian forces during the Jacobite Rising of 1745-6.

   The castle is reportedly haunted by a ghost in a green dress, the *Ell-maid of Dunstaffnage,* and her appearance heralds events, both bad and good, in the lives of the Campbells.

✆ 01631 562465—Open April to September

 P S 🚻 £ ♿ 🚻

67 Duntrune Castle

Off B8025, 6.5 miles NW of Lochgilphead, Argyll
NR 794956   OS: 55

Duntrune Castle, originally a 13th-century castle of enclosure, has a 16th-century tower house at one corner.

   It was a property of the Campbells of Duntrune. The castle was besieged in 1645 after the Battle of Inverlochy, when the lands of the Campbells were ravaged by the Marquis of Montrose's army. It was burnt by the Earl of Argyll in 1685, but was sold in 1792 to the Malcolms of Poltalloch, who still own it.

   Duntrune is reportedly haunted by a ghostly piper. In the 17th century,

a piper from a band of
MacDonalds had been sent
as a spy to try to capture the
castle from the Campbells.
He was discovered, caught
and imprisoned in one of
the chambers. The only way
he could warn the rest of
his band was to play the
bagpipes. Both his hands
were cut off in revenge, and
his ghost began to haunt
the castle.

The ghost was thought to have been exorcised in modern times, when
part of the basement was used as a church. A handless skeleton was
supposedly found sealed behind a wall, and the remains buried; and two
skeleton hands were reportedly also discovered under the kitchen floor.
However, the ghost became active again, and in the 1970s unexplained
knockings on doors were reported, as well as furniture and other objects
being thrown about the rooms – although the piper's apparition and the
skirl of pipes are also supposed to have been heard.

68 Duntulm Castle

Off A855, 6.5 miles N of Uig, Skye, Highland
NG 410743   OS: 23

On a strong site, once cut off on the landward side by a ditch, Duntulm is
now a very ruinous castle. It was built by the MacDonalds, and was
formerly a comfortable and lordly residence.

Hugh MacDonald was imprisoned and starved to death in a dungeon
here after he had tried to seize the lands of Trotternish by murdering his
kin. He was given only salted beef and no water, and died raving. His
ghost then reputedly haunted the dungeon.

Another spirit was said to be one of the chiefs, Donald Gorm, brawling
and drinking – as he had done while alive – although now with spectral
companions.

Yet another was Margaret, a sister of MacLeod of Dunvegan, who was
married to Donald MacDonald of Duntulm. She had lost an eye in an

accident, and her husband spurned her, sending her back to Dunvegan on a one-eyed horse, accompanied by a one-eyed servant, and a one-eyed dog. Her weeping ghost is said to have been witnessed here.

A careless nursemaid is also said to have dropped a baby out of one of the windows, onto the rocks below, and reputedly her terrified screams can still sometimes be heard.

One story suggests that the MacDonalds moved to nearby Monkstadt, itself now a ruin, because of the ghosts.

Open all year – ruin in a dangerous condition

69 Durris House

Off B9077, 6.5 miles E of Banchory, Aberdeenshire

NO 799968   OS: 45

Durris House, an altered and extended 16th-century tower house, is now divided into flats. It was held by the Frasers from the 13th century, and was burned by the Marquis of Montrose in 1645. The *Green Lady*, said to haunt the house, dates from this time, and was wife of the Fraser lord. She is said to have cursed Montrose during his visit, and he torched the house in revenge. Her curse may have had some effect, however, as Montrose was defeated finally in 1650, captured and taken to Edinburgh where he was executed.

70 Earlshall

Off A919, east of Leuchars, Fife

NO 465211   OS: 59

Earlshall, a picturesque courtyard castle, consists of a main block, a smaller detached tower, and a range of outbuildings around the courtyard. On the second floor is a gallery with a tempera-painted ceiling from the 1620s. The castle was abandoned and became ruinous, before being restored by the architect Sir Robert Lorimer in 1892.

Sir William Bruce built the castle in 1546 – he was one of the few to survive the Battle of Flodden in 1513. One of the family was Sir Andrew Bruce, known as *Bluidy Bruce*, for his persecution of Covenanters. He and his men killed Richard Cameron at Airds Moss in 1680, hacking off Cameron's head and hands, and taking them back to Edinburgh, where they were brought before the council. Bruce's apparition is said to haunt the castle, and ghostly footsteps have been heard here.

71 Edinburgh Castle

Off A1, in Edinburgh

NT 252735 OS: 66

Standing on a high rock, Edinburgh Castle was one of the strongest and most important castles in Scotland and, although most of the present complex of buildings dates from no earlier than the 15th century, has a long and bloody history.

There was a fortress on the castle rock from earliest times, but the oldest building is a small Norman chapel of the early 12th century, dedicated to St Margaret, wife of Malcolm Canmore, and built by her son, David I. The castle was held by the English from 1296 until 1313 when the Scots, led by Thomas Randolph, climbed the rock, surprised the garrison, and retook it. It was slighted, but there was an English garrison here again until 1341, when it was retaken by a Scot's force disguised as merchants bringing provisions to the garrison. In 1367-71 David II rebuilt the castle with strong walls and towers.

After the murder of the young Earl of Douglas and his brother at the *Black Dinner* at the castle in 1440, it was attacked and captured by the Douglases after a nine-month siege and required substantial repairs.

In 1566 Mary, Queen of Scots, gave birth to the future James VI in the castle. After her abdication, it was held on her behalf, but surrendered in 1573. Cromwell besieged it throughout the autumn of 1650. It is the home to the Scottish crown jewels and Stone of Destiny, Mons Meg – a large 15th-century cannon – and offers spectacular views over the capital.

The castle is reputedly haunted by many ghosts, including a drummer seen when the castle is about to be attacked, a ghostly piper who disappeared searching tunnels beneath the castle and the High Street, and the spectre of a dog whose remains are buried in the pets' cemetery.

☎ 0131 225 9846—Open all year; courtesy vehicle can take visitors with disabilities to Crown Square

🅿 (except during Tattoo) ☕ S 🚾 ⅃ ♿ 🚾/Facilities

72 Eilean Donan Castle

Off A87, 8 miles E of Kyle of Lochalsh, Highland

NG 881259 OS: 33

One of the most beautifully situated of all castles, Eilean Donan consists of a 13th-century wall surrounding a courtyard. In one corner stands a

strong 14th-century keep with a gabled roof and parapet.

Alexander III gave the lands to Colin Fitzgerald, son of the Irish Earl of Desmond and Kildare, for his help in defeating King Haco at the Battle of Largs in 1263. The family changed their name to Mackenzie, and Eilean Donan became their main stronghold. Robert the Bruce sheltered here in 1306. In 1331 Randolph, Earl of Moray, executed 50 men and *decorated* the walls with their heads. William Mackenzie, 5th Earl of Seaforth, had Eilean Donan garrisoned with Spanish troops during the Jacobite Rising of 1719, but three frigates battered it into submission, and it was blown up from within. The Spanish were defeated at the nearby Battle of Glenshiel. Although very ruinous, Eilean Donan was rebuilt and restored in the 19th century.

The spirit of one of the Spanish troops, killed either at the castle or the nearby battle, is said to haunt the castle.

☎ 01599 555202—Open April to 1 November

P S WC ⚭

73 Ethie Castle

Off A92, 5 miles NE of Arbroath, Angus

NO 688468 OS: 54

Once a fortress of some strength, Ethie Castle consists of a large keep, dating from the 15th century, and probably incorporating older work. It was greatly extended in later centuries, and is still occupied.

Ethie was a property of the Beatons in the 16th century, and was used by Cardinal David Beaton when he was Abbot of Arbroath in the 1530s, and later when he was Archbishop of St Andrews. Beaton was murdered in 1546, and his ghost is said to haunt the castle.

Another ghost was reportedly that of a child – heard running about and playing with toys – which mostly haunted one particular chamber. The skeleton of an infant was apparently later found in this room, and when the remains were buried, this haunting is said to have ceased.

74 Fedderate Castle

Off A981, 2 miles NE of New Deer, Aberdeenshire
NJ 897498   OS: 30

Little remains of Fedderate Castle, a large tower house which was once surrounded by a moat. The castle was built by the Crawford family, later passed to the Gordons, and is said to be haunted.

75 Ferniehirst Castle

Off A68, 1.5 miles S of Jedburgh, Borders
NT 653179   OS: 80

Ferniehirst Castle, built about 1476 by the Kerrs, consists of an extended tower house, forming one corner of a large house. Sir Thomas Kerr supported Mary, Queen of Scots, and invaded England in 1570, hoping to have her released – but all that resulted was a raid by the English in reprisal during which Ferniehirst was damaged. James VI sacked the castle in 1593. A *Green Lady* is said to haunt the castle.

76 Finavon Castle

Off A94, 4.5 miles NE of Forfar, Angus
NO 497566   OS: 54

Once a strong and important castle, Finavon Castle consists of a ruined tower house, dating from the 14th-century. It was held by the Lindsay Earls of Crawford from 1375. David, 3rd Earl, and his brother-in-law, Ogilvie of Inverquharity, were badly wounded at the Battle of Arbroath in 1446, and were brought back to the castle. The Earl soon died and his wife suffocated Ogilvie – her own brother – with a pillow to ensure the succession of her own son, Alexander. Alexander became 4th Earl, and was called *The Tiger* or *Earl Beardie*, a cruel and ruthless character, who is said to haunt two castles – Lordscairnie and Glamis – himself. He hung from hooks a minstrel who correctly foretold of the Lindsays defeat at the Battle of Brechin in 1452. Crawford fled after the battle, but James II pardoned him. On the Covin Tree, grown from a chestnut dropped by a Roman soldier, Crawford hung Jock Barefoot for cutting a walking stick from the tree, and Jock's ghost is said to haunt the castle.

77 Frendraught Castle

Off B9001, 6 miles E of Huntly, Aberdeenshire
NJ 620418   OS: 29

Frendraught Castle, a property of the Crichtons, was burnt out in 1630 during a feud with the Gordons. Twelve guests, including the Lord of Rothiemay and Lord Aboyne, both from the Gordon family, were burned and killed in the castle – although the Crichton hosts escaped. Crichton of Frendraught was tried, but acquitted of their murder, only one of his servants was executed. The spirit of Lady Elizabeth Crichton, a *White Lady*, who may have been involved in the torching, is said to have been seen here, even in the 20th century, usually on the stairs. Other manifestations include cries, running footsteps and screams.

 The present gabled house with a rectangular tower, dates mostly from 1656 after the burning of the castle. It was remodelled in 1753, extended in 1790, and incorporates part of the old 13th-century castle. The house was restored in 1974, and is still occupied.

78 Fyvie Castle

Off A947, 1 mile N of Fyvie village, Aberdeenshire
NTS   NJ 764393   OS: 29

Incorporating work from the 13th century, Fyvie is one of the most splendid castles in Scotland. The main block is known as the Seton Tower, and three other large towers – the Preston, Meldrum and Gordon towers – each refer to the family which built it. The wide main turnpike stair is decorated with 22 coats of arms. Many of the chambers are panelled in wood, and have plaster ceilings and tempera painting.

 Fyvie was originally a property of the Lindsays. Edward I of England stayed here in 1296, as did Robert the Bruce in 1308. The property

passed to the Prestons, Meldrums, the Seton Earls of Dunfermline, the Gordons, and then to the Leith family – but is now owned by the National Trust for Scotland. There is a garden.

The castle is reputedly haunted by several ghosts. One, the *Grey Lady* is believed to be the spectre of a lady starved to death here. The ghost was at her most active in the 1920s and 1930s. When workmen were renovating one of the rooms, they found a secret chamber behind a wall in which was the skeleton of a woman. When the skeleton was removed, disturbances increased until it was reputedly returned to the secret chamber.

Another ghost is said to be the *Green Lady*, an apparition of Lilias Drummond – wife of Alexander Seton, first Earl of Dunfermline – who died on 8 May 1601. Her appearance bodes ill for the family, and she is recorded as often being seen on the main turnpike stair. She may have been starved to death by her husband, or have died of a broken heart, as Seton married Lady Grizel Leslie only four months after her death. Lilias's ghost is said to have scratched her name on the stone window sill of the newlyweds' bedroom, the *Drummond Room*, on the night of 27 October 1601, soon after they were married – and the writing can still be seen.

Some say the castle also has a ghostly drummer, while others a trumpeter – nearly enough to make up a band.

☎ 01651 891266—Castle open April to September; weekends only in October; grounds open all year

P S WC £ ♿ Facilities

79 Galdenoch Castle

Off B738, 6 miles W of Stranraer, Dumfries & Galloway
NW 974633   OS: 82

Galdenoch Castle, a ruined tower house, was built by Gilbert Agnew, who was killed at the Battle of Pinkie in 1547. The castle is said to have been haunted at one time, and the spirit made a habit of grabbing old women and throwing them into water. The ghost is said to have been exorcised by the mighty singing of a priest.

80 Garth Castle

Off B846, 6 miles W of Aberfeldy, Perthshire
NN 764504   OS: 52

Standing on a steep crag, Garth Castle is a plain 14th-century keep, with a strong iron yett. It was built by Alexander Stewart, the *Wolf of Badenoch*, Lord of Badenoch and Earl of Buchan, illegitimate son of Robert II. He torched Elgin Cathedral and town, as well as Forres, after being excommunicated by the Bishop of Elgin for deserting his wife. He died in 1396, and is buried in Dunkeld Cathedral.

In 1502 Nigel Stewart of Garth attacked nearby Weem Castle, burned it, and took Sir Robert Menzies prisoner. Stewart put Menzies in the vaulted dungeon at Garth, threatening to have him killed unless he sign away his lands. Stewart was nearly executed for the crime, only the intervention of the Earl of Atholl saving him. Later suspected of murdering Mariota, his wife – whose apparition is said to have been seen here – Stewart was imprisoned at Garth until his death in 1554.

81 Gight Castle

Off B9005, 4 miles E of Fyvie, Aberdeenshire
NJ 827392   OS: 29

Gight Castle is a ruined tower house and courtyard, built by the Gordons in the 1570s. In the 18th century, Catherine Gordon married John Byron, but in 1787 had to sell Gight to pay off his gambling debts. Their son was the poet Lord Byron.

Ghostly bagpipes can reputedly be heard from the castle. A piper was ordered to explore a tunnel under the castle, but never returned and was not seen again. Only his pipes supposedly continued – and continue – to be heard.

82 Glamis Castle

Off A928, 5.5 miles SW of Forfar, Angus

NO 387481 OS: 54

One of the most famous – and supposedly haunted – castles in Scotland, Glamis Castle consists of a 14th-century keep, extended with wings and towers in later centuries. The great hall, a fine chamber with a large fireplace, is on the second floor, and there is a garden. Robert the Bruce

gave the lands to the Lyon family, and in the 15th century they were held by Sir John Lyon, Chancellor of Scotland, who married a daughter of Robert III. The castle is still held by the same family, now Earls of Strathmore and Kinghorne, and was the childhood home of Her Majesty Queen Elizabeth the Queen Mother.

In 1540 the young and beautiful wife of the 6th Lord, Janet Douglas, was burned to death on a false charge of witchcraft by James V, who hated the Douglases. Her spirit, the *Grey Lady of Glamis* is said to haunt the castle.

Another ghost associated with the castle is believed to be Alexander Lindsay 4th Earl of Crawford, *Earl Beardie,* who is said to haunt a walled-up room where he played cards – or diced, depending on the version of the story – with the devil.

Other recorded ghosts include a little Negro boy, who sits on a stone seat in the hall. Ghostly cries are said to be heard from a party of Ogilvies who were starved to death in one of the chambers after seeking refuge from a band of Lindsays. A *White Lady* is said to haunt the castle clock tower. An apparition of a bearded man, starved to death here in 1486, has also supposedly been seen.

☎ 01307 840393—Open 28 March to 26 October

P ☕ S wc & 𝒞 wc/Access to gardens

83 Grandtully Castle

Off A827, 2.5 miles NE of Aberfeldy, Perthshire

NN 891513   OS: 52

Built by the Stewarts in the 14th century, Grandtully Castle is an altered and extended tower house, to which has been added a large mansion, in the same style, in 1893. The castle was used by the Marquis of Montrose; General Mackay; the Earl of Argyll; the Earl of Mar in the Jacobite Rising of 1715; and Bonnie Prince Charlie in the 1745 Rising. Following an earlier Jacobite Rising – after defeat of government forces at the Battle of Killiecrankie in 1689 – a soldier killed an officer in one of the angle-turrets. The blood staining the floor was said to be permanently visible.

84 Grange House

Off A7, 1.5 miles S of Edinburgh Castle

NT 262716   OS: 66

Grange House, an extended and remodelled 16th-century tower house, was completely demolished in 1936. Bonnie Prince Charlie stayed here in 1745. The house reputedly had many ghosts, one a miser, who from time to time rolled a barrel of gold through the house.

85 Hallgreen Castle

Off A92, E of Inverbervie, Aberdeenshire

NO 832721   OS: 45

Hallgreen Castle, a much-altered 16th-century tower house of the Rait family, may incorporate earlier work and has been extended by a modern mansion. The old part has steep roofs, angle-turrets and corbiestepped gables. The castle has been recently restored and is occupied

Several ghosts are said to haunt the castle, including two medieval serving girls, a woman who reputedly killed herself after the death of her child, and a cloaked man.

86 Hermitage Castle

Off B6357, 5 miles N of Newcastleton, Borders
His Scot NY 497960 OS: 79

One of the most impressive and oppressive of Scottish fortresses, Hermitage Castle consists of a strong 13th-century walled courtyard and large 14th-century keep.

The property belonged to the Dacres, but passed to the De Soulis family. One of the family, *Bad Lord Soulis,* was a man of ill repute and was said to dabble in witchcraft. Many local children were siezed by Soulis and never seen again. The local people eventually rebelled, and Soulis was wrapped in lead and boiled in a cauldron, or simply immersed head-first into a vat of lead, depending on the version of the tale. However, it is more likely he was merely imprisoned in Dumbarton Castle for supporting the English: the family lost the castle and lands in 1320. Ghostly screams and cries can sometimes reputedly be heard from the victims of Lord Soulis.

The castle later passed to the Douglas family. William Douglas, *The Knight of Liddesdale*, was prominent in resisting Edward Balliol in the 1330s. He seized Sir Alexander Ramsay of Dalhousie, however, while at his devotions, and imprisoned him in a dungeon at Hermitage, and had him starved to death, although it seems to have taken a long time as some grain seeped into the prison from a store above. The ghost of Ramsay is said to have been both seen and heard within the walls. In 1353 Douglas, himself, was murdered by his godson, another William Douglas, after he had tried to block his rightful claim to the lordship of Douglas.

The castle was acquired by the Earls of Bothwell. In 1566 James Hepburn, 4th Earl of Bothwell, was badly injured in a skirmish with the Border reiver Wee Jock Elliot, and while recovering from his wounds was paid a visit by Mary, Queen of Scots. Mary and Bothwell later married, but he had to flee to Norway after defeat at the Battle of Carberry Hill in 1567. Bothwell was eventually imprisoned in the Danish castle of Dragsholm until his death. An apparition of Mary, clad in a white dress, is said to haunt the castle.

☎ 01387 376222—Open April to September daily but weekends only September to March

 P S ♿

87 Holyroodhouse

Off A1, 1 mile E of Edinburgh Castle
His Scot NT 269739 OS: 66

Holyrood Abbey was founded by David I around 1128, and James III preferred the comfortable guest range of the abbey to the starker Edinburgh Castle. James IV and James V both extended and remodelled the palace.

David Rizzio – Mary, Queen of Scots's secretary – was murdered in her presence here by men led by her husband, Henry Stewart, Lord Darnley. The spot where his body lay is helpfully marked by a pool of *blood*.

A *Grey Lady*, thought to be the spirit of one of Mary's companions, has reputedly been seen in the Queen's Audience chamber. Ghostly footsteps have been reputedly heard in the long gallery, which has portraits of Scottish monarchs, most of them entirely fictitious.

Holyroodhouse, the official residence of the monarch in Scotland, consists of ranges of buildings, one dating from the 16th century, enclosing a courtyard. The ruins of the Abbey church adjoin the Palace.

☎ 0131 556 1096—Open all year except during Queen's residence
🅿 Nearby **S** &

88 Huntingtower Castle

Off A9, 2 miles NW of Perth railway station
His Scot NO 083252 OS: 58

A well-preserved and interesting castle, Huntingtower consists of a 15th-century keep, an adjacent 16th-century tower house, and a later small connecting range. Some rooms have fine mural paintings and plaster work, as well as decorative painted beams.

The castle was built by the Ruthvens, later Earls of Gowrie, and was called Ruthven Castle. Mary, Queen of Scots, visited the castle in 1565

while on honeymoon with Lord Darnley, although the 3rd Lord Ruthven, Patrick, took part in the murder of Rizzio, Mary, Queen of Scots's secretary. In 1582 the Earl of Gowrie kidnapped the young James VI in the *Raid of Ruthven* and held him in Huntingtower for a year, until the King escaped during a hunting trip. In 1600, however, the Earl of Gowrie and his brother, Alexander, Master of Ruthven, were murdered in Gowrie House in Perth by James VI, following the *Gowrie Conspiracy*, a possible plot to murder the king. The Ruthven's property was confiscated, and the name of the castle changed to Huntingtower.

The space between the tower and keep is known as *The Maiden's Leap*. A daughter of the Earl of Gowrie was visiting her lover in his chamber. In imminent danger of being found by her mother, the girl had no option but to leap the gap from the keep to the tower house, and then returned to her own bed before being discovered.

The castle and grounds are said to be haunted by a *Green Lady*: *My Lady Greensleeves*. Her footsteps are reputedly heard along with the rustle of her gown, and she has reputedly appeared on several occasions, sometimes as a warning of death, sometimes to help passers-by.

📞 01738 627231—Open all year except closed Thur PM and Fri October to March

 P S ♿

88 Inchdrewer Castle

Off A97, 3 miles SW of Banff, Aberdeenshire

NJ 656607 OS: 29

Inchdrewer Castle, an altered 16th-century tower house, was built by the Ogilvies of Dunlugas, later Lords Banff, in the 16th century. In 1713 Lord Banff was murdered in the castle after unexpectedly returning home from Edinburgh. He was probably killed by his own servants, who had been robbing him and who set the building alight to destroy any evidence. The castle is said to be haunted.

89 Inveraray Castle

Off A83, N of Inveraray, Argyll

NN 096093 OS: 56

The present imposing castle, built by the Campbell Earls – and Dukes – of Argyll in 1743, is a symmetrical neo-classical mansion. The house contains many interesting rooms, with collections of tapestries, paintings

and furniture, and displays of weapons. Rob Roy MacGregor's sporran and dagger handle are on show.

A ghostly harper, one of Montrose's victims of the attack in 1644, is said to haunt the castle, although this would have been at the earlier stronghold nearby, which is not on the same site. The *Green Library* is also reputedly haunted, and strange noises and crashes have been heard there. Other ghosts include a spectral birlinn – a small galley – which is reportedly seen when one of the Campbells is near death; and the ghost of a young servant, who was murdered and dismembered by Jacobites.

☎ 01499 302203—Open April to June & September to mid-October Sat to Thurs; July & August daily

P ☕ S wc ⅃ ♿ Access to ground floor only

90 Jedburgh Castle

Off A68, in Jedburgh, Borders

NT 647202 OS: 74

Site of a 12th-century stronghold, where Malcolm the Maiden – Malcolm IV King of Scots – died in 1165. Alexander III was married here in 1285, but a ghostly apparition warned of his impending death – which came true when Alexander fell from a cliff while riding at Kinghorn during a storm. This apparition was apparently seen many times, and was always the harbinger of death. The castle was occupied by the English from 1346 until 1409, when it was retaken by the Scots and finally demolished.

91 Kellie Castle

Off B9171, 4 miles N of Elie, Fife

NTS NO 520052 OS: 59

One of the finest castles in Scotland, Kellie Castle is a 16th-century tower house, consisting of a main block with three large square towers forming an 'E'. There is a fine garden.

An earlier castle here belonged to the Sewards, but the present castle was built by the Oliphants, who held the lands from 1360 until 1613 when the 5th Lord Oliphant had to sell the property. It was bought by Sir Thomas Erskine of Gogar, made Earl of Kellie in 1619, a favourite of James VI. Erskine was involved in the *Gowrie Conspiracy* and may have been one of those who murdered the Master of Ruthven and his brother, the Earl of Gowrie.

Kellie was abandoned in 1829, but in 1878 James Lorimer, Professor of Public Law at Edinburgh University, leased Kellie as an almost roofless ruin and proceeded to restore it. He died in 1890, and his ghost is said to

have been seen seated in one of the passageways. The famous architect Robert Lorimer, his son, spent most of his childhood at Kellie. In 1970 Kellie passed into the care of the National Trust for Scotland.

A turnpike stair in the castle is reputedly haunted by the spirit of Anne Erskine, who died by falling from one of the upstairs windows. The sound of her feet on the steps has supposedly been heard often.

☎ 01333 720271—Open Easter weekend; open May to September; open weekends only in October; grounds open all year

 Facilities

92 Kindrochit Castle

Off A93, S of Braemar, Aberdeenshire
NO 152912 OS: 43

Not much remains of a once strong castle with square corner towers. It was reputedly destroyed when plague broke out among those in the castle, and the folk of Braemar imprisoned them inside. Cannons were used to bring down the walls, and kill anyone remaining alive.

A tale about the castle is that in 1746 a Hanoverian soldier was lowered into one of the vaults in search of treasure, but fled when he found a ghostly company seated around a table piled with skulls – alternatively he may just have been scared and – not wanting to look a coward – made up a frightening story. During excavations nothing supernatural was found, but the *Kindrochit Brooch* was discovered.

Open all year

Kindrochit Castle – see above

93 Kinnaird Castle

Off A934, 5.5 miles W of Montrose, Angus

NO 634571   OS: 54

Kinnaird, a 19th-century mansion which was further enlarged in 1854-60 by the architect David Bryce, incorporates the basement of a 15th-century castle. It was a property of the Carnegies, and Walter Carnegie of Kinnaird fought at the Battle of Brechin in 1452 against the Earl of Crawford, although the castle was later burnt in revenge. The Carnegies were made Earls of Southesk in 1633. The house is still occupied.

One story connected with the castle is that the corpse of James Carnegie, the 2nd Earl of Southesk, who died in 1669, was taken by a ghostly black coach driven by black horses – and that this apparition has appeared more than once. Carnegie is said to have studied in Padua, where he learnt much black magic – and where he managed to lose his shadow – and that the devil had come to collect his own when Carnegie died.

94 Kinnaird Head Castle

Off A98, N of Fraserburgh, Aberdeenshire

NJ 999677   OS: 30

Kinnaird Head Castle consists of an altered massive 15th-century keep. A lighthouse was built into the top of the castle in 1787, and the outbuildings were built around it in 1820 by Robert Stevenson, grandfather of Robert Louis Stevenson. It now forms part of Scotland's lighthouse museum.

The *Wine Tower*, standing about 50 yards away, is a lower tower, now of three storeys, all of them vaulted.

The castle was a property of the Frasers of Philorth. Sir Alexander Fraser built the harbour at Fraserburgh – the town formerly called Faithlie. After coming near near to bankrupting himself, Fraser had to sell much of his property in 1611. Fraser had his daughter's lover – of whom he disapproved – chained in a sea cave below the *Wine Tower*, where the poor man drowned during a gale. His daughter, Isobel, threw herself to her death on finding that her lover had been killed. An apparition is said to been seen by the *Wine Tower* whenever there is a storm.

☎ 01346 511022—Open all year

🅿 ☕ S 🚾 ₤ ♿ Access to museum

95 Lauriston Castle

Off B9085, 3 miles W of Edinburgh Castle

NT 204762   OS: 66

Lauriston Castle, a much-altered tower house with later extensions, was built by the Napiers of Merchiston. One of the family, John Napier, was

the inventor of logarithms. The castle passed through several families to the Reids, who were the last owners and gave it to the city of Edinburgh in 1926. The castle has some good interiors, although the ghostly sound of feet has reportedly been heard here.

☎ 0131 336 2060—Open daily April to October except Fri; grounds open all year

P WC ᏻ ♿ WC/Access to grounds

96 Linlithgow Palace

Off A803, in Linlithgow, West Lothian
NT 003774 OS: 65

Once a splendid palace and still a spectacular ruin, Linlithgow Palace consists of ranges of buildings set around a rectangular courtyard, and may include 12th-century work. There is a fine carved fountain in the middle of the courtyard.

There was a 12th-century castle here which was captured and strengthened by Edward I of England in 1301. It was slighted after being retaken by the Scots by driving a cart under the portcullis.

It was mostly rebuilt by James I at the beginning of the 15th century, and became a favourite residence of the kings of Scots, the work continuing under James III, James IV, and James V, who was born here in 1512 as was Mary, Queen of Scots, in 1542. *Queen Margaret's Bower*, at the top of one of the stair-towers, is said to be haunted by Mary of Guise, waiting for the return of her husband, James V.

After the Union of the Crowns in 1603, the palace was left in charge of a keeper. It was last used by Charles I in 1633, although his son, James, Duke of York, stayed here before succeeding to the throne in 1685. In 1746 General Hawley retreated here after being defeated by the Jacobites at the nearby Battle of Falkirk. The soldiers started fires to dry themselves, and the palace was accidentally set blaze. It was never restored.

The palace is also said to be haunted by a *Blue Lady*, who walks from the entrance of the palace to the nearby parish church of St Michael. It was in the parish church that a blue-robed apparition warned James IV not to march into England – but the king ignored the warning, invaded England, and was killed at the disastrous Battle of Flodden in 1513.

☎ 01506 842896—Open all year

 S ₤

97 Littledean Tower

Off A699, 6.5 miles W of Kelso, Borders
NT 633314   OS: 74

Littledean Tower, a ruined 16th-century tower and later unusual D-plan tower, was a property of the Kerrs. In earlier days, it was said to be the birth place of *Dun Scotus*, John of Duns, who won renown as an eminent scholar from some, and the name *dunce* from others. The castle was burnt in 1544 by the English.

A ghostly horsemen, the spirit of one of the Kerr lords, is said sometimes to be seen near the castle. A cruel man, he scorned his wife and friends, and is said to have become involved with a witch, whose severed hand eventually strangled him in his own bed.

98 Loch Leven Castle

Off B996, 1 mile E of Kinross, Perthshire
NO 138018   OS: 58

Loch Leven was a royal castle from 1257, but by the end of the 14th century had passed to the Douglases of Lochleven. Archibald, 5th Earl of Douglas, was imprisoned and died here in 1439, as did Patrick Graham, Archbishop of St Andrews, in 1477. Mary, Queen of Scots – held here from 1567 until she escaped in 1568 – signed her abdication during her captivity, possibly after a miscarriage, and she is said to haunt the castle. The ruined remains include a small 15th-century keep, standing at one corner of a 14th-century courtyard. The stronghold used to occupy most of the island, but the level of the loch has been lowered.

☎ 01786 450000—Open April to September; ferry out to island from Kinross

P S wc ₤ ♿ wc

99 Loch of Leys

Off A980, 1 mile N of Banchory, Aberdeenshire

NO 700980 OS: 45

Site of a 14th-century castle of the Burnetts on a former island in the now drained loch. Alexander Burnett of Leys married Janet Hamilton in 1543, and acquired a sizeable dowry of church lands. With this new wealth, they built Crathes Castle – a splendid tower house – and abandoned Leys.

The old castle was reputedly haunted. Alexander Burnett fell in love with Bertha, a relative who was staying at the castle. His mother, Agnes, wanted a more advantageous match for her son, and poisoned Bertha. Agnes was apparently frightened to death by a spectre of Bertha, and an apparition is said to still appear on the anniversary of Bertha's death.

Lordscairnie Castle – see next page

100 Lordscairnie Castle

Off A913, 3 miles NW of Cupar, Fife

NO 348178   OS: 59

Lordscairnie Castle, a 15th-century keep, had a courtyard of which only a single round tower of a gatehouse survives. It was a property of the Lindsay Earls of Crawford from around 1350, and it was probably the 4th Earl, Alexander *Earl Beardie* or the *Tiger Earl*, who built the castle. It was abandoned in the 18th century, but there is reputedly treasure buried near the ruins.

The castle is said to be haunted by Alexander Lindsay, *Earl Beardie* , who can be seen playing cards with the devil on the stroke of midnight of New Year's Eve – this may be a *transplanted* story from Glamis.

101 Loudon Castle

Off A719, 1 mile N of Galston, Ayrshire

NS 506378   OS: 70

Loudon Castle, a large ruined mansion, incorporates a tower house dating from the 15th century. The original tower was a property of the Crawfords, but passed to John Campbell, Chancellor of Scotland, who was made Earl of Loudon in 1641. The property later passed to Francis, Lord Hastings, who built much of the mansion, although he ran out of money. The castle was used by Belgian troops during World War II, and in 1941 was accidentally torched and gutted. It remains a large impressive ruin, and is now the centre piece of a theme park with a park, woodland, fairground and museum.

The castle was reputedly haunted for many years by a *Grey Lady*, whose apparition was apparently seen many times before the fire in 1941.

☎ 01563 822296—Loudon Castle Park open April to October

🅿 ⬛ S 🚾 £ ♿ 🚾/Limited access

102 Macduff's Castle

Off A955, N of East Wemyss, Fife

NT 344972   OS: 59

Macduff's Castle consists of a ruined 14th-century keep and courtyard, although there may have been a castle here of the MacDuff Thanes or Earls of Fife in the 11th century. The existing castle was built by the

Wemyss family in the 14th century. In 1666 the Countess of Sutherland, who was a daughter of the 2nd Earl of Wemyss, kept her children here during a plague in Edinburgh.

The ghost of a woman, the *Grey Lady,* is said to haunt the castle. She is said to be Mary Sibbald, who was found guilty of thievery and died as a result of her punishment.

Open all year – ruins may be in a dangerous condition

103 Mains Castle

Off B783, 1 mile N of East Kilbride, Lanarkshire

NS 627560   OS: 64

Mains Castle is a fine plain keep with a parapet, dating from the 15th century. The lands were held by the Lindsays of Dunrod from the 14th century. In 1306, one of the family – along with Kirkpatrick of Closeburn– helped finished off John Comyn the Red in a church in Dumfries after Robert the Bruce had stabbed him. A later Lindsay, while curling on the ice of a nearby loch and angered by one of his servants, had a hole cut, and drowned the unfortunate man by forcing him under the ice. The property was sold because of debt about 1695, and the castle unroofed in 1723 to become ruinous. It has since been restored.

The apparition of a woman, strangled by her jealous husband, has reputedly been seen at Mains.

104 Marlfield House

Off B6401, 5.5 miles S of Kelso, Borders

NT 735255   OS: 74

Marlfield House, possibly designed by William Adam, incorporates part of a castle dating from the 17th century or before. The house is said to be haunted by a ghost that pushes past people in one of the passageways, and has reputedly been active in recent years.

105 Meggernie Castle

Off B846, 8 miles N of Killin, Perthshire

NN 554460   OS: 51

Meggernie Castle is a tower house, built by Colin Campbell of Glenlyon, with a steep roof and angle-turrets. It later passed to Menzies of Culdares. James Menzies of Culdares, *Old Culdares* was a Jacobite who took part in the Rising of 1715, and sheltered Jacobite fugitives here while entertaining Hanoverian troops during the 1745 Rising. The castle was later remodelled and extended, and is still occupied.

Meggernie is reputedly haunted by the top half and lower half of a woman, which has apparently been seen many times, both in the castle and in the grounds. She is said to be the ghost of the beautiful wife of one of the Menzies lords of the 17th or 18th century. He was a very jealous man, and in a fit murdered her, cutting her in half, hoping to dispose of her body later. Her top half haunts the upper floors, where this part of her body was hidden; while her bloodied lower half is seen on the ground floor and near the family burial ground, where this part of her was later reputedly buried. During renovation towards the end of the 19th century, the upper bones of her skeleton were discovered, but the haunting continued even after her remains were buried.

106 Melgund Castle

Off B9134, 4.5 miles SW of Brechin, Angus
NO 546564   OS: 54

Melgund Castle is a tower house with later ranges of buildings – currently

being restored – was originally built in the 16th century by Cardinal David Beaton, Archbishop of St Andrews and Chancellor of Scotland. He was murdered at St Andrews in 1546, and his ghost has reputedly been seen at the castle. Melgund passed to the Gordon Marquis of Huntly in the 17th century, then to the Maules, then

the Murrays, Earls of Minto and Viscounts Melgund.

107 Menie House

Off A92, 2 miles N of Balmedie, Aberdeenshire

NK 978206   OS: 38

Menie House, a two-storey Jacobean house of about 1840, incorporates an 18th-century house at one corner, and stands on the site of a 15th-century castle.

The castle is said to be haunted by a *Green Lady*, who is said to have been seen in the basement of the old part.

108 Muchalls Castle

Off A92, 4 miles NE of Stonehaven, Aberdeenshire

NO 892908   OS: 45

Little altered and well preserved, Muchalls Castle is an early 17th-century courtyard castle, built by the Burnetts, but incorporating older work. The hall, on the first floor, is a fine chamber with a painted plaster ceiling and a large fireplace, with a coloured overmantel, which is dated 1624. Other chambers also have painted ceilings, and there is a secret stair.

The castle is reputedly haunted by the ghost of young woman, the *Green Lady*, who was drowned in a cave, which formerly could be reached by a subterranean stair from the wine-cellar. She had been awaiting her lover, but somehow slipped into the water and was killed. Her ghost, clad in a green gown, has been seen in some of the chambers, sometimes sitting in front of a mirror.

109 Neidpath Castle

Off A72, 1 mile W of Peebles, Borders

NT 236405   OS: 73

Standing on a steep bank of the River Tweed, Neidpath Castle is an altered keep, with rounded corners, dating from the 14th century. A small courtyard with ranges of buildings – one of which now houses a museum – were added in the 16th and 17th centuries.

An earlier castle here belonged to Sir Simon Fraser. He defeated the English at Roslin Glen in 1302, but was later captured and executed. The property passed to the Hays, who built the existing castle. James VI stayed at Neidpath in 1587. In 1650 Neidpath held out against Cromwell's forces longer than any other stronghold south of the Forth. Cannon damaged the castle, and the defenders were eventually forced to surrender.

The ghost of a young woman, a *White Lady,* is said to have been seen at Neidpath. She had fallen in love with a local laird, but her father did not think the man good enough, and forbade them to marry. The girl was heartbroken, and languished to become sick and weak. Finally relenting as he feared she might die, her father allowed the marriage, but the girl had so deteriorated that her lover no longer recognised her. She died soon afterwards, and her sad apparition is said to haunt the castle.

☎ 01721 720333—Open Thur before Easter to September

🅿 S ⅃ ♿ Access to museum/ground floor only

110 Newton Castle

Off A923, NW of Blairgowrie, Perthshire

NO 172453 OS: 53

Standing in a strong position, Newton Castle is a 16th-century Z-plan tower house, although it may incorporate a older work. It was a property of the Drummonds, who feuded with the Blairs of nearby Ardblair. The tower was sacked by the Marquis of Montrose in 1644, and burnt by Cromwell, although the defenders of the tower are supposed to have survived in the vaults, while the building burned around them.

Newton is said to be haunted by a *Green Lady*, dressed in green silk, who searches through the castle, as she is said to do at Ardblair as well. One version of the story is that it is the spirit of Lady Jean Drummond of Newton, who had fallen in love with one of the Blairs of Ardblair. The families feuded and Lady Jean seems to have pined away with a broken heart, when she was betrothed to another, until she drowned herself in a local loch.

An old ballad tells a slightly different story, that Jean had consulted a local witch after her lover had spurned her. Jean was given an enchanted green dress, which won him back, but died shortly after marrying him.

111 Noltland Castle

Off B9066, NE side of island of Westray, Orkney
His Scot   HY 430487   OS: 5

A strong and grim stronghold, Noltland Castle is a large ruined Z-plan tower house, dating from the 16th century, and built by the Balfours. Gilbert Balfour, Master of the Household to Mary, Queen of Scots, was involved in the murders of Cardinal Beaton in 1546 – for which he was imprisoned – and Lord Darnley in 1567. Some of the Marquis of Montrose's men took refuge here after defeat in 1650, and the castle was later held by Cromwell's men. Noltland was abandoned about 1760.

A death in the Balfour family was reputedly heralded by a ghostly howling dog here, while births and marriages were announced by a strange spectral light. The castle is also said to have had a brownie, a helpful spirit which undertook many household chores and other work.
Open all year

112 Old Woodhouselee Castle

Off B7026, 1.5 miles NE of Penicuik, Midlothian
NT 258617   OS: 66

Not much survives of a 16th-century tower house of the Hamiltons, except cellars and a ruined wing.

Lady Hamilton of Bothwellhaugh and her young child were stripped naked and turned out of their home here by the order of Regent Moray about 1570. The baby died and Lady Hamilton went mad, and died soon afterwards. Her husband, James Hamilton of Bothwellhaugh, shot and killed Regent Moray in 1570 at Linlithgow. Hamilton was later executed. The castle was dismantled in the late 17th century, and materials used to build Woodhouselee, itself demolished in 1965. The ruins were said to be haunted by the ghost of Lady Hamilton, dressed in white, searching for her baby, and her spirit seems to have been witnessed at

Woodhouselee as well. Her apparition was apparently seen frequently at one time.

113 Penkaet Castle

Off A6093, 1 mile SW of Pencaitland, East Lothian
NT 427677   66

Standing in a walled garden, Penkaet Castle is a picturesque rambling tower house, dating from the 16th century. Originally a property of the Maxwells, it then passed to the Cockburns and the Pringles. The name was changed to *Fountainhall* after it was sold in 1685 to the Lauders. In recent years the name has been changed to *Penkaet Castle*.

Penkaet is reputedly haunted by several ghosts. One is said to be the spectre of Alexander Hamilton, a beggar, who cursed the family. He was accused of witchcraft after the lady of the house and her eldest daughter died from a mysterious illness. He was tried, found guilty and executed in Edinburgh.

Another spirit manifests itself by banging doors and moving furniture, and is thought to be the spirit of one of the Cockburns.

A four-poster bed, once belonging to Charles I, is reputedly haunted in that it often appears to have been slept in, although it has not been used.

Manifestations have been reported in the 20th century, and the house was investigated in the 1920s, and many unexplained noises and events were recorded.

114 Pinkie House

Off A199, in Musselburgh, Edinburgh
NT 353727   OS: 66

Pinkie House, an altered 16th-century house, was built by the Setons and added to in later centuries. One of the family was Alexander Seton first Earl of Dunfermline, and Chancellor to James VI. He died at the house in 1622, and it is his first wife, Lilias Drummond – the *Green Lady* – who is thought to haunt Pinkie – as well as Fyvie Castle. Her appearance is said to bode ill for the family.

Charles I stayed here, as did Bonnie Prince Charlie following victory over Sir John Cope and his army at Prestonpans in 1745 during the Jacobite Rising. The house is part of Loretto, a private boarding school for boys.

115 Pitcaple Castle

Off A96, 4 miles NW of Inverurie, Aberdeenshire
NJ 726261   OS: 38

Pitcaple Castle is a tower house, dating partly from the 15th century, remodelled in the 19th century. The castle was formerly surrounded by a walled courtyard with a gatehouse, drawbridge and moat.

The lands were held by the Leslies from 1457. James IV stayed here, as did Mary, Queen of Scots, in 1562. Charles II visited in 1650, and the then laird was killed at the Battle of Worcester, fighting for Charles, in 1651.

When a robin is found in the castle it is reputedly the harbinger of bad news and the herald of death – one was discovered when the laird was killed at the Battle of Worcester in 1651, and there are apparently other occasions when this was also the case.

116 Rait Castle

Off A939, 2.5 miles S of Nairn, Highland
NH 894525   OS: 27

Rait Castle is a ruined castle of the Rait family, most of which dates from a 13th-century hall-house. The Duke of Cumberland stayed here before victory at the Battle of Culloden against the Jacobites in 1746. The castle is reputedly haunted by the ghost of a young woman, wearing a blood-stained dress.

117 Rockhall

Off A75, 6 miles E of Dumfries
NY 054754   OS: 85

Rockhall is a plain tower house, held from the 15th century by the Griersons of Lag. Sir Robert Grierson, persecutor of Covenanters, lived here. His pet monkey, killed by his servants after his death, is said to haunt the house, blowing a whistle.

118 Roslin Castle

Off B7006, 2 miles S of Loanhead, Midlothian
NT 274628   OS: 66

Once a formidable and splendid fortress, Roslin Castle consists of a ruined round keep and ranges of buildings and towers. Standing on a high bank above a river, Roslin was the main stronghold of the Sinclair

Earls of Orkney and Caithness, who lived like princes. During the Wars of Independence, an English force was heavily defeated in 1302 by the Scots near the castle, led by Simon Fraser and John Comyn the Red. A ghost of a dog, killed with its English master after the battle, reputedly haunts the castle, and its howling has been reported.

Sir William Sinclair, who probably built the keep, was one of the knights who set out on a Crusade with Robert the Bruce's heart and was killed fighting the Moors in Granada in 1330. Roslin was accidentally burnt in 1452, and was torched by the English in 1544, and in 1650 by Cromwell.

Roslin Chapel, once a Collegiate Church, was founded by William Sinclair, Earl of Caithness and Orkney, in 1446 and is open to the public. In the burial vault are interred ten of the Earls of Roslin and their kin, said to be in full armour.

119 Roxburgh Castle

Off A699, 1 mile W of Kelso, Borders

NT 713337   OS: 74

Not much remains of a courtyard castle, first built by David II in the 12th century, once one of the main strongholds of Scotland. It was occupied by the English during the Wars of Independence, until retaken by the Scots under James Douglas in 1314. In 1460 James II was killed when one of the guns with which he was bombarding the castle blew up beside him, but the castle was stormed and demolished. A ghostly horsemen is said to be seen sometimes seen riding towards the castle near from where James was killed.

120 Ruthven Barracks

Off A9, 1 mile S of Kingussie, Highland

His Scot NN 764997 OS: 35

Nothing remains of a 13th-century castle of the Comyns, which was later held by Alexander Stewart, the *Wolf of Badenoch*, as the chief stronghold of his lordship. In 1451 it passed to the Gordon, Earl of Huntly, but in that year was sacked by John MacDonald, Earl of Ross. Mary, Queen of Scots visited the castle. In 1718 the castle was completely demolished after being damaged in 1689, and was replaced by a barracks for Hanoverian troops. It was held by government forces in 1746, but was eventually taken and burnt by Jacobite forces.

Alexander Stewart, the *Wolf of Badenoch*, illegitimate son of Robert II, was made Lord of Badenoch and then Earl of Buchan – this by his own hand by forcing the Countess of Buchan to marry him. He was responsible for the burning of Elgin Cathedral and town and Forres – after he had been excommunicated. He reputedly dabbled in witchcraft, but in 1396 a visitor to the castle, dressed all in black, challenged Stewart to a game of chess. In the morning there was nobody left alive for Stewart had reputedly played with the devil. The shades of Stewart and his followers, still playing chess, are said to haunt the place – or so the story goes – although Stewart was buried in Dunkeld Cathedral.

Open all year

121 Saddell Castle

Off B842, 8 miles N of Campbeltown, Argyll

NR 789316 OS: 68

The castle stands on what were church lands of Saddell Abbey – there is said to be a ghostly monk at the castle – founded by Reginald, son of Somerled in the 12th century. The lands passed to the Bishops of Argyll, who around 1507 built a stronghold, although in 1559 it was sacked by the Earl of Sussex. A *White Lady* reputedly walks the battlements,

The castle consists of an altered 15th-century keep with a range of 18th-century outbuildings, which replaced the original courtyard. It was restored in the 20th century

122 St Andrews Castle

Off A91, in St Andrews, Fife
His Scot NO 513169 OS: 59

Standing close to the remains of the cathedral, St Andrews Castle is a ruined courtyard castle of the Bishops of St Andrews, and there is an exhibition and visitor centre nearby.

The first fortress here was built by Bishop Roger, but was dismantled by Robert the Bruce around 1310. It was rebuilt in 1336 by the English in support of Edward Balliol, but was captured by Sir Andrew Moray, the Regent, in 1337 and slighted again. At the end of the 14th century, Bishop Trail rebuilt the castle once again. Patrick Graham, the first Archbishop, was deposed and imprisoned both here and at Lochleven in 1477. Archbishop Alexander Stewart was killed at Flodden in 1513.

Cardinal David Beaton strengthened the castle by adding two round blockhouses, now destroyed. However, in 1546 a band of Reformers stole into the castle and murdered Beaton, hanging his naked body from one of the windows. This was partly in revenge for the burning by Beaton of the Protestant preacher, George Wishart, for heresy. Reinforced by others, including John Knox, the Reformers held the castle for a year. The besiegers tunnelled towards the walls, and the defenders counter-mined and captured their tunnel. Both tunnels still survive.

A ghost is said to haunt the castle, which may have been Archbishop Hamilton, who was hanged at Stirling in 1571. He had supported Mary, Queen of Scots, but was captured with the fall of Dumbarton Castle. Alternatively, it may be the spirit of Cardinal Beaton, who is also said to haunt both Melgund and Ethie castles, as well as the road to St Andrews.

☎ 01334 477196—Open all year; combined ticket available for Castle and Cathedral

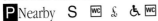 **P** Nearby S WC ⚬ ♿ WC

123 Saltoun Hall

Off B6355, 5 miles SW of Haddington, East Lothian
NT 461685 OS: 66

Saltoun Hall, a later mansion, incorporates part of a castle dating from as early as the 12th century. Saltoun was occupied by the English in 1547, led by Cockburn of Ormiston, but was retaken by the Earl of Arran for the

Scots in a surprise attack. It was sold in 1643 to Sir Andrew Fletcher of Saltoun, *The Patriot*, who was prominent in resisting the Union of parliaments of Scotland and England in 1707. The hall is divided into flats and is occupied.

It is reputedly haunted by a *Grey Lady*.

124 Sanquhar Castle

Off A76, 0.25 miles S of Sanquhar, Dumfries & Galloway
NS 786092 OS: 78

Sanquhar Castle is a ruined castle, dating from the 13th century. A tower stands at one corner, and a ruined hall block and later wing also survive.

The lands passed to the Crichtons in the 14th century. Two ghosts reputedly haunt the castle. One is the *White Lady*, possibly the spirit of a young fair girl, Marion of Dalpeddar, who is thought to have disappeared about 1590. She may have been murdered by one of the Crichton lords, and a skeleton of a girl was found in 1875 during excavations. Another ghost is said to be John Wilson, wrongly hanged by one of the Crichtons.

In 1639 the castle was sold to Sir William Douglas of Drumlanrig, who was later made Duke of Queensberry. The Duke had Drumlanrig Castle built, but only spent one night in his new mansion, decided he did not like it, and moved back to Sanquhar. However, his son moved to Drumlanrig, and Sanquhar was abandoned to become ruined.
Open all year

125 Shieldhill

Off B7016, 3 miles NW of Biggar, Lanarkshire
NT 008407 OS: 72

A castle, dating from as early as 1199, of the Chancellor family has been incorporated into a sprawling building, mostly 16th century, of many styles. It was extended in the 17th century, and again in 1820, and is now used as a hotel.

The building is said to be haunted by the ghost of a daughter of a Chancellor lord. She was raped by soldiers returning from a battle towards the end of 17th century, and became pregnant, but the child was taken from her at birth and left to die. The girl wept herself to death, and her ghost has reputedly been seen in the hotel, even in recent times.
Hotel – open all year and to non-residents.

126 Skibo Castle

Off A9, 4 miles W of Dornoch, Sutherland

735891 OS: 21

The present Skibo Castle, a massive 19th-century baronial mansion, was built for Andrew Carnegie, but stands on the site of an old castle. This old

castle was reputedly haunted by the ghost of a young woman. She was a girl, who was entertained here by a servant of the castle, but was afterwards never seen – in life – again. She appears to have been murdered, and the apparition of a partially dressed young woman has been witnessed, as well as screams and cries. A skeleton was later found hidden behind a wall, and when buried, the hauntings apparently ceased.

127 Spedlins Tower

Off A74, 3 miles NE of Lochmaben, Dumfries & Galloway

NY 098877 OS: 78

Spedlins Tower, a tower house dating from the 15th century, was built by the Jardines. The tower was abandoned – for nearby Jardine Hall, a 19th-century house – and became ruinous, but was restored and reoccupied in the 1960s.

Spedlins was haunted by the ghost of a miller called Porteous, who had the misfortune to be imprisoned here. The then laird, Sir Alexander Jardine, forgetting about his prisoner, was called away to Edinburgh and took the key to the dungeon with him. No food could be got to the miller, and Porteous gnawed at his feet and hands before eventually dying of hunger. Disturbances then followed, with cries and shouts from the prison and other manifestations. The ghost was *kept quiet* by keeping a bible near the dungeon, but when it was removed it is said that the ghost followed the family to Jardine Hall. The disturbances apparently stopped after Spedlins Tower became a ruin.

128 Stirling Castle

Off A872, in Stirling
His Scot NS 790940 OS: 57

One of the most important and powerful castles in Scotland, Stirling Castle, standing on a high rock, is a courtyard castle, partly dating from the 12th century. The *King's Old Building* contained royal chambers, and the *Chapel Royal* is where Mary, Queen of Scots, was crowned.

The earliest recorded castle at Stirling was used by Malcolm Canmore. Alexander I died here in 1124, as did William the Lyon in 1214. Edward I of England captured the castle in 1304 when he used – although after the garrison had surrendered: Edward was like that – a siege engine called the *War Wolf*. William Wallace siezed the castle for the Scots, but it was

retaken by the English, until after the Battle of Bannockburn in 1314. Robert the Bruce had the castle slighted, but it was rebuilt by Edward III of England.

The English garrison was besieged in 1337 by Andrew Moray, the Regent, but it was not until 1342 that the Scots recovered the castle. The future James III was born here in 1451.

James II lured the 8th Earl of Douglas to Stirling in 1452, murdered him, and had his body tossed out of one of the windows. Mary, Queen of Scots, was crowned in the old chapel in 1533. James VI stayed here in 1617, as did Charles I in 1633, and Charles II in 1650. In 1651 the castle was besieged by Monck for Cromwell, but it surrendered after a few days. The garrison harried the Jacobites during both the 1715 and 1745 Risings. After 1745, the castle was subdivided to be used as a barracks, but in 1964 the army left. There is a visitor centre, gardens and exhibitions.

The *Pink Lady*, the apparition of a beautiful woman in a pink silk gown, has reportedly been seen at the castle, and may be the ghost of Mary, Queen of Scots. Another story is that she is the ghost of a woman searching for her husband, who was killed when the castle was captured by Edward I. The *Green Lady's* appearance is sometimes a warning of bad events to follow, often associated with fire. She may have been one of the ladies of Mary, Queen of Scots – said to have saved Mary when her bedclothes caught fire – and has reportedly been seen in recent times.

☎ 01786 450000—Open all year

129 Sundrum Castle

Off A70, 4.5 miles E of Ayr, Ayrshire

NS 410213   OS: 70

Sundrum Castle, a Georgian mansion of 1793, incorporates a much-altered 14th-century keep of the Wallaces. The castle is said to be haunted by a *Green Lady*.

130 Taymouth Castle

Off A827, 5 miles W of Aberfeldy, Perthshire

NN 785466   OS: 52

Taymouth Castle, a large 19th-century mansion, replaced a tower house built by Sir Colin Campbell of Glenorchy around 1580.

It was a property of the Campbells, who were made Earls of Breadalbane in the late 17th century. The castle is reputedly haunted, and ghostly footsteps have been heard here.

Taymouth Castle – see previous page

131 Traquair House

Off B709 or B7062, 1 mile S of Innerleithen, Borders
NT 330354 OS: 73

Reputedly one of the oldest continuously inhabited houses in Scotland,
Traquair House is an altered and extended tower house, which may
incorporate work from as early as the 12th century. Attractions include a
working 18th-century brewery, garden and maze, and craft workshops.

The property had passed to the Stewarts in 1478. Mary, Queen of Scots,
visited with Lord Darnley in 1566 – she left behind a quilt, possibly
embroidered by her and her four Marys. Bonnie Prince Charlie stayed in
the house in 1745, entering through the Bear Gates. One story is that the

7th Earl closed and locked them after Charlie's departure, swearing they would not be unlocked until a Stewart once more sat on the throne of the country; another that they were locked after the death of the Earl's young wife and were not to be opened until he remarried – which he never did. They are still locked. The house has a collection of Stewart mementoes, not least the ghost of Bonnie Prince Charlie, who is said to have been seen between the Bear Gates and the house. Another ghost seen in the grounds is reportedly the spirit of Lady Louisa Stewart, who died in 1871 when she was 100.

☎ 01896 830323—Open daily Easter to September; open Fri, Sat & Sun only in October

/Limited access to house

132 Woodhouselee

Off A702, 2.5 miles N of Penicuik, Midlothian
NT 238645   OS: 66

The mansion of Woodhouselee was built in the late 17th century when the property was held by the Purves family, but incorporated part of an old tower house. It is said that the mansion was haunted by a ghost of Lady Hamilton of Bothwellhaugh, apparently having come from Old Woodhouselee.

133 Wemyss Castle

Off A955, 3 miles NE of Kirkcaldy, Fife
NT 329951   59

Wemyss Castle consists of an altered rectangular keep and large courtyard, which enclosed ranges of buildings. The castle was extended and the courtyard was filled in by the end of the 19th century. Most of the Victorian additions were demolished in the 1930s.

   The castle was built by the Wemyss family, who were made Earls in 1631, and still live at the castle. Mary, Queen of Scots, first met Lord Darnley – later her second husband – here in 1565.

   A *Green Lady* reputedly haunts the castle, and is said to have been seen in many parts of the building.

Glossary

Angle-Turret A turret crowning corners of a building

Arcade   A series of arches supported by piers or columns.

Arch   A self-supporting structure capable of carrying a load over an opening

Attic   The top storey entirely within a gabled roof

Bailey   A defensible area enclosed by a wall or palisade and a ditch

Basement   The lowest storey of a building, sometimes below ground level

Battlement A crenellated parapet to shoot between the solid sections

Caphouse   A small watch-chamber at the top of a turnpike stair, often opening into the parapet walk and sometimes rising from within the parapet

Castle   A fortified house or stronghold, residence of a nobleman

Castellations Battlements and turrets

Corbiestepped *(Scots)* Squared stones forming steps upon a gable

Corbel   A projecting bracket supporting other stonework or timbers

Courtyard castle Usually a castle of some size and importance built around a central courtyard, with a tower or keep, gatehouse, and ranges of buildings such as a kitchen, bakehouse, stable and chapel

Crenellations Battlements

Crowstepped   Squared stones forming steps upon a gable (corbiestepped)

Curtain Wall A high enclosing stone wall around a bailey

E-plan tower house Tower house with a main block and at least two wings at right angles, dating from the 16th and 17th centuries

Enceinte   The line of the wall encircling a fortress

Gable   A vertical wall or other vertical surface, frequently triangular, at the end of a pitched roof, often with a chimney. In Scotland often corbiestepped (crowstepped)

Gallery   A balcony or passage, often with seats, usually overlooking a great hall or garden

Garret   The top storey of a building within the roof

Keep   Strong stone tower. A citadel or ultimate strong point, normally with a vaulted basement, hall and additional storeys. Often with very thick walls, a flush parapet, and mural chambers. Dates from the 14th and 15th centuries. Originally called a donjon

L-plan tower house Distinctive Scottish form of the tower house in which a wing was added at right angles to the main tower block, thereby affording greater protection by covering fire and providing more accommodation. Dates between 1540–1680

Main Block Principal part of a castle, usually containing the hall and lord's chamber

Moat   A ditch, water filled or dry, around an enclosure

Motte   A steeply sided flat-topped mound

Motte and bailey A defence system, Roman in origin, consisting of an earth motte (mound) carrying a wooden tower with a bailey (open court) with an enclosing ditch and palisade

Palace   An old Scottish term for a two-storey hall block

Parapet   A wall for protection at any sudden drop, but defensive in a castle

Pit-Prison   A dark prison only reached by a hatch in a vault

Portcullis   A wooden and/or iron gate designed to rise and fall in vertical grooves

Postern   A secondary gateway or doorway; a back entrance

Rampart   A stone or earth wall surrounding a castle

Royal castle A castle held by a keeper or constable for the monarch

Scale-and-platt Stair with short straight flights and turnings at landings

Slight   To destroy a castle's defences to a greater or lesser extent

Tempera   Form of wall painting directly onto wet plaster

Tower House Self-contained house with the main rooms stacked vertically usually with a hall over a vaulted basement with further storeys above. Normally in a small courtyard, or barmkin. Dating from 1540 to about 1680

T-plan   House or tower where the main (long) block has a wing or tower (usually for the stair) in the centre of one front

Turnpike stair Spiral stair around a newel or central post

Turret   A small tower usually attached to a building

Vault   An arched ceiling of stone

Yett   A strong hinged gate made of interwoven iron bars

Walled Enclosure A simple castle, normally where a wall encloses a rock or island with a wooden hall and buildings. Dates from the 12th and 13th centuries (castle of enceinte, castle of enclosure)

Z-plan   Distinctive Scottish form of the tower house where two corner towers were added to the main tower block at diagonally opposite corners, thereby affording greater protection by covering fire and providing more accommodation. Dates from the 16th and 17th centuries

Index

Adamson family, 32
Agnew family, 51
Airds Moss, Battle of, 19, 45
Alexander III, 46, 58
animal (monkey or other), 38, 46, 72
Arbroath, Battle of, 48

Baillie, William, 23
Balfour family, 70
Bannockburn, Battle of, 78
Black Dinner, 35, 46
Blair family,12, 69
Beaton, Cardinal David, 6, 29, 47, 67, 70, 75
beggar's curse, 71
Blue lady, 5, 18, 63
Bonnie Prince Charlie, *see* Stewart, Charles Edward, 6, 36-7, 43, 53, 71, 80
Bothwell, James Earl of, *see* Hepburn, James, 20, 35, 54
Boyd, Earls of Kilmarnock, 18, 37
Brahan Seer (Kenneth Mackenzie), 21
Brown, John, 17
brownie, 33, 70
Bruce, Robert, King of Scots, 2, 34, 47, 49, 52, 66, 73, 75, 78
Buchanan family, 22
Burnett family, 34, 64, 68

Caithness, Earls of, 26
Cameron family, 45
Cameronians, 19
Campbell family, 43
Campbell, Earls of Argyll, 28-9, 39, 43, 57
Campbell, Earls of Loudon, 65
Campbell of Glenlyon, 66
Campbell, Sir Duncan of Glenorchy, 17, 18, 79
cannon ball, 22
Carberry, Battle of, 54
Carbisdale, Battle of, 13
Cardinal Beaton, *see* Beaton, Cardinal David, 6, 29, 47, 67, 70, 75
Carnegie, Earls of Southesk, 6, 60
Cathcart family, 6, 23
Chancellor family, 76
Charles I, 63, 71, 79
Charles II, 19, 32, 41, 72, 79

Clearances, 42
Cockburn family, 71, 75
Comyn family, 41, 66, 74
Corrichie, Battle of, 38
Covenanters, 6, 13, 19, 23-4, 41, 45, 72
Crawford family, 48
Crichton family, , 49, 76
Cromwell, Oliver, 13, 19, 32, 41, 68-70, 73
Culloden, Battle of, 36-7, 72
Cumberland, Duke of, 36, 72

Dalrymple family, 15
Dalziel family, 6, 18
Darnley, Lord, Henry Stewart, 55-6, 70, 80
David I, 46
David II, 46, 73
devil, 5-6, 14, 19, 52, 60, 65, 74
Douglas family, 2, 33, 35, 38-44, 52, 54, 63
Drummond family, 6, 12, 50, 69, 71
drummer, 6, 31, 50
Dunbar family, 6, 15

Earl Beardie, *see* Lindsay, Alexander, 4th Earl of Crawford, 5-6, 49, 52, 65
Edward I of England, 49, 62, 78
Edward III of England, 41, 78
Elizabeth, the Queen Mother, 26, 52
Erskine of Gogar, Earls of Kellie, 58
Erskine, Earls of Mar, 20

Falkirk, Battle of, 63
Farquharson, John of Inveray, 21
Flodden, Battle of, 40, 45, 63, 75
Forbes family, 30, 32, 36
Forrester family, 31
Fraser family, 12, 45, 61, 68

Galbraith family, 35
Gordon family, 11, 16, 30, 32, 38, 42, 48, 50-1, 67-8
Gowrie Conspiracy, 56, 58
Graham family, 20, 22
Graham, James, Marquis of Montrose, 13, 24, 38, 43, 45, 53, 57, 69
Graham of Claverhouse, John, 29
Grant family, 16, 25
Green lady, 5-6, 12, 14-16, 26, 28, 30, 34, 43, 45, 48, 50, 56, 68-9, 71, 79, 81

Grierson family, 72
Grey lady, 5, 12, 17, 21, 50, 52, 55, 65-6, 76
Gunn family, 11

Hamilton family, 6, 21, 32, 64, 70, 81
harper, 57
Hay family, 28, 43
Hay, Earls of Errol, 38
Hepburn, James, Earl of Bothwell, 20, 35, 54
Hepburn family, 35
horsemen, 6, 26, 35, 39, 73
hounds, 6, 18, 73

Jacobite Rising(1715), 20, 24-5, 40, 53, 67, 79
Jacobite Rising(1745), 25, 31, 37, 39, 43, 67, 71-2, 79
James I, 62
James II, 49, 73, 78
James III, 37, 62, 78
James IV, 15, 40, 43, 55, 62-3, 72
James V, 52, 55, 62-3
James VI (and I), 38, 46, 48, 56, 58, 68, 71, 79
James VII (and II), 63
Jardine family, 77

Keith family, 2, 11, 49
Kennedy of Culzean, 23, 36
Kerr family, 48, 63
Killiecrankie, Battle of, 29, 53
Knox, John, 29, 75

Langside, Battle of, 29, 32
Lauder family, 71
Leslie family, 72
Lindsay, Earls of Crawford, 48, 60, 65
Lindsay, Alexander, 4th Earl of Crawford, 5-6, 49, 52, 65
Lindsay family, 49
Lindsays of Dunrod, 66
Livingstone family, 24
Lorimer, James, 58
Lorimer, Sir Robert, 45, 59
Lundie family, 15
Lyle family, 40
Lyon family, 52

MacDonald family, 44

MacDonald, Lords of the Isles, 31
MacDougall of Lorn, 24, 43
MacDuff family, 65
MacGregor, Rob Roy, 15, 57
Mackenzie, Earls of Seaforth, 21, 47
Mackenzie of Tarbat, 23
Mackintosh family, 26
MacLaine family, 6, 26, 39
MacLean family, 6, 26, 39
Macleod family, 13-14, 44
Macpherson family, 14
Malcolm Canmore, 46, 78
Malcolm IV, 58
Malcolms of Poltalloch, 43
Mary, Queen of Scots, 6, 15, 20, 29, 32-3, 35, 38, 41, 46, 48, 54-6, 62-3, 70, 72, 74-5, 78-80, 83
Maxwell family, 71
Meldrum family, 50
Menzie family, 51, 66
Montgomery family, 13
Moray, Earls of, 26, 41, 75, 78
Mortimer family, 32
Morton family, 25
Mowbray family, 18
Munro family, 6, 17
Mure family, 30
Murray, Earls of Annandale, 30

Napier family, 61
Nimmo family, 31

Ogilvie, Earls of Airlie, 31, 48, 52
Ogilvie, Earls of Findlater, 36
Ogilvie of Dunlugas, Lord Banff, 57
Oliphant family, 12, 58
Otterburn, Battle of, 13

Philiphaugh, Battle of, 38
Pink lady, 5, 79
Pinkie, Battle of, 51
piper, 6, 35-6, 43-4, 46, 51
playing cards/dice/chess, 5-6, 19, 52, 65, 74
Preston family, 50
Pringle family, 6, 22, 71
Primrose family, 18

Rait family, 53, 72
Ramsay family, 54
Randolph, Earls of Moray, 35

Regent Moray, 33, 70

Reid family, 62

Rizzio, David, 55-6

Rob Roy MacGregor, *see* MacGregor Rob
    Roy, 15, 57

Robert the Bruce, *see* Bruce, Robert, King
    of Scots, 2, 34, 47, 49, 52, 66, 73, 75, 78

Ross family, 17

Rullion Green, Battle of, 19

Ruthven family, 56

Seton family, 50, 71

Seward family, 58

Sibbald family, 15

Sinclair family, 42, 72-3

Soulis family, 5-6, 54

Spalding family, 14

Stark family, 14

Stewart, Alexander, Wolf of Badenoch, 6,
    51, 74

Stewart, Charles Edward, 6, 36-7, 43, 53, 71,
    80

Sutherland, Earls of, 42

trumpeter, 50

unrequited love, 4-5, 11-12, 14-16, 21, 25-6,
    29-30, 42, 61, 64, 68-9

Urquhart family, 35

Victoria, Queen, 11, 17

Wallace family, 79

Wallace, William, 12-13, 41, 78

Wars of Independence, 12, 21

Wemyss family, 81

White deer, 6, 22

White lady, 3, 5, 25, 29, 31, 49, 53, 69, 74, 76

William and Mary, 29

witchcraft, 5, 11, 17, 52, 54, 70-1, 74

Wolf of Badenoch, *see* Stewart, Alexander,
    6, 51, 74

Worcester, Battle of, 19, 72